CliffsNotes™

Heart of Darkness and The Secret Sharer

By Dan Moran

D0010980

IN THIS BOOK

- Use the exclusive CliffsNotes icons to guide you

- Character analysis and visual enhancements show you the psychological motivations and interrelationships of major characters

- Summaries and Commentaries that complement each other so you can learn the quick and easy way

- Includes life and times of the author to illustrate how these events shaped the author's writing

- Learn more about the author's work or just supplement your current understanding

- Reinforce what you learn with CliffsNotes Review

- Find additional information to further your study in CliffsNotes Resource Center and online at www.cliffsnotes.com

Hungry Minds™

Best-Selling Books • Digital Downloads • e-Books • Answer Networks • e-Newsletters • Branded Web Sites • e-Learning
New York, NY • Cleveland, OH • Indianapolis, IN

About the Author
Dan is a high school teacher and has won many teaching awards.

Publisher's Acknowledgments
Editorial
Project Editor: Sherri Fugit
Acquisitions Editor: Greg Tubach
Copy Editor: Rowena Rappaport

Editorial Assistant: Laura Jefferson
Editorial Administrator: Michelle Hacker
Glossary Editors: The editors and staff of Webster's New World Dictionaries

Production
Indexer: York Production Services, Inc.
Proofreader: York Production Services, Inc.
Hungry Minds Indianapolis Production Services

CliffsNotes™ *Heart of Darkness* and "The Secret Sharer"
Published by:
Hungry Minds, Inc.
909 Third Avenue
New York, NY 10022
www.hungryminds.com
www.cliffsnotes.com (CliffsNotes Web site)

ISBN: 0-7645-8584-3

Printed in the United States of America

10 9 8 7 6 5 4 3

1O/QR/QS/QS/IN

Distributed in the United States by Hungry Minds, Inc.

Library of Congress Cataloging-in-Publication Data
Moran, Daniel, 1968-
    CliffsNotes on Conrad's Heart of Darkness and The Secret Sharer / by Daniel Moran.
        p. cm.
    Includes bibliographical references.
    ISBN 0-7645-8584-3 (alk. paper)
    1. Conrad, Joseph, 1857-1924. Heart of Darkness
-Examinations--Study guides. 2. Conrad, Joseph,
1857-1924. Secret Sharer--Examinations--Study
guides. 3. Psychological fiction, English--History and
criticism. I. Title: Conrad's Heart of Darkness. II.
Title: Heart of Darkness, III. Title: Secret Sharer. IV.
Title.
PR6005.O4 H4778 2000
823'.912--dc21
                                                   00–039691

Distributed by CDG Books Canada Inc. for Canada; by Transworld Publishers Limited in the United Kingdom; by IDG Norge Books for Norway; by IDG Sweden Books for Sweden; by IDG Books Australia Publishing Corporation Pty. Ltd. for Australia and New Zealand; by TransQuest Publishers Pte Ltd. for Singapore, Malaysia, Thailand, Indonesia, and Hong Kong; by Gotop Information Inc. for Taiwan; by ICG Muse, Inc. for Japan; by Norma Comunicaciones S.A. for Columbia; by Intersoft for South Africa; by Eyrolles for France; by International Thomson Publishing for Germany, Austria and Switzerland; by Distribuidora Cuspide for Argentina; by LR International for Brazil; by Galileo Libros for Chile; by Ediciones ZETA S.C.R. Ltda. for Peru; by WS Computer Publishing Corporation, Inc., for the Philippines; by Contemporanea de Ediciones for Venezuela; by Express Computer Distributors for the Caribbean and West Indies; by Micronesia Media Distributor, Inc. for Micronesia; by Grupo Editorial Norma S.A. for Guatemala; by Chips Computadoras S.A. de C.V. for Mexico; by Editorial Norma de Panama S.A. for Panama; by American Bookshops for Finland. Authorized Sales Agent: Anthony Rudkin Associates for the Middle East and North Africa.

For general information on Hungry Minds' products and services please contact our Customer Care department; within the U.S. at 800-762-2974, outside the U.S. at 317-572-3993 or fax 317-572-4002.

For sales inquiries and resellers information, including discounts, premium and bulk quantity sales and foreign language translations please contact our Customer Care department at 800-434-3422, fax 317-572-4002 or write to Hungry Minds, Inc., Attn: Customer Care department, 10475 Crosspoint Boulevard, Indianapolis, IN 46256.

For information on licensing foreign or domestic rights, please contact our Sub-Rights Customer Care department at 212-884-5000.

For information on using Hungry Minds' products and services in the classroom or for ordering examination copies, please contact our Educational Sales department at 800-434-2086 or fax 317-572-4005.

Please contact our Public Relations department at 212-884-5163 for press review copies or 212-884-5000 for author interviews and other publicity information or fax 212-884-5400.

For authorization to photocopy items for corporate, personal, or educational use, please contact Copyright Clearance Center, 222 Rosewood Drive, Danvers, MA 01923, or fax 978-750-4470.

Hungry Minds™ is a trademark of Hungry Minds, Inc.

Table of Contents

How to Use This Book

CliffsNotes *Heart of Darkness* and *The Secret Sharer* supplements the original work, giving you background information about the author, an introduction to the novel, a graphical character map, critical commentaries, expanded glossaries, and a comprehensive index. CliffsNotes Review tests your comprehension of the original text and reinforces learning with questions and answers, practice projects, and more. For further information on Joseph Conrad and *Heart of Darkness* and *The Secret Sharer* check out the CliffsNotes Resource Center.

CliffsNotes provides the following icons to highlight essential elements of particular interest:

Reveals the underlying themes in the work.

Helps you to more easily relate to or discover the depth of a character.

Uncovers elements such as setting, atmosphere, mystery, passion, violence, irony, symbolism, tragedy, foreshadowing, and satire.

Enables you to appreciate the nuances of words and phrases.

Don't Miss Our Web Site

Discover classic literature as well as modern-day treasures by visiting the Cliffs-Notes Web site at www.cliffsnotes.com. You can obtain a quick download of a CliffsNotes title, purchase a title in print form, browse our catalog, or view online samples.

You'll also find interactive tools that are fun and informative, links to interesting Web sites, tips, articles, and additional resources to help you, not only for literature, but for test prep, finance, careers, computers, and the Internet, too. See you at www.cliffsnotes.com!

LIFE AND BACKGROUND OF THE AUTHOR

Personal Background

Joseph Conrad, one of the English language's greatest stylists, was born Teodor Josef Konrad Nalecz Korzenikowski in Podolia, a province of the Polish Ukraine. Poland had been a Roman Catholic kingdom since 1024, but was invaded, partitioned, and repartitioned throughout the late eighteenth-century by Russia, Prussia, and Austria. At the time of Conrad's birth (December 3, 1857), Poland was one-third of its size before being divided between the three great powers; despite the efforts of nationalists such as Tadeusz Kosciuszko, who led an unsuccessful uprising in 1795, Poland was controlled by other nations and struggled for independence. When Conrad was born, Russia effectively controlled Poland.

Conrad's childhood was largely affected by his homeland's struggle for independence. His father, Apollo Korzeniowski, belonged to the *szlachta*, a hereditary social class comprised of members of the landed gentry; he despised the Russian oppression of his native land. At the time of Conrad's birth, Apollo's land had been seized by the Russian government because of his participation in past uprisings. He and one of Conrad's maternal uncles, Stefan Bobrowski, helped plan an uprising against Russian rule in 1863. Other members of Conrad's family showed similar patriotic convictions: Kazimirez Bobrowski, another maternal uncle, resigned his commission in the army (controlled by Russia) and was imprisoned, while Robert and Hilary Korzeniowski, two fraternal uncles, also assisted in planning the aforementioned rebellion. (Robert died in 1863 and Hilary was imprisoned and exiled.) All of this political turmoil would prove to be predictably disturbing to young Josef, who could only stand idly by as he watched his family embroiled in such dangerous controversy. The notion of the strong oppressing the weak—and the weak powerless to revolt—surfaces in *Heart of Darkness*, where the White traders wantonly murder the Congolese in pursuit of riches and power.

Conrad's father was also a writer and translator, who composed political tracts, poetry, and satirical plays. His public urgings for Polish freedom, however, eventually caused Russian authorities to arrest and imprison him in 1861; in 1862, his wife (Conrad's mother), Eva, was also arrested and charged with assisting her husband in his anti-Russian activities. The two were sentenced to exile in Vologda, a town in northern Russia. Their exile was a hard and bitter one: Eva died of tuberculosis in 1865 and Apollo died of the same disease in 1869. Conrad, now only twelve years old, was naturally devastated; his own physical health deteriorated and he suffered from a number of lung inflammations and epileptic seizures. His poor health would become a recurring problem throughout the remainder of his life. Poland did not gain independence until 1919, and although patriots such as Apollo were instrumental in this eventual success, their martyrdom left many children (such as Conrad) without parents or hope for their future.

The Call of the Sea

After his father's death, Conrad was returned to Krakow, Poland where he became a ward of his maternal uncle, Thaddeus Bobrowski. His uncle sent Conrad to school in Krakow and then to Geneva under the guidance of a private tutor. However, Conrad was a poor student; Despite his having studied Greek, Latin, mathematics, and (of course) geography, he never completed the formal courses of study that he was expected to finish. His apathy toward formal education was counter-balanced by the reading he did on his own: During his early teenage years, Conrad read a great deal, particularly translations Charles Dickens' novels and Captain Frederick Marryat, an English novelist who wrote popular adventure yarns about life at sea. (He also read widely in French.)

Marryat's novels may have been partly responsible for the sixteen-year-old Conrad's desire to go to sea and travel the world as a merchant marine (an exotic wish for a boy who grew up in a land-locked country); in 1874, his uncle reluctantly granted him permission to leave Poland and travel, by train, to the French port city of Marseille to join the French Merchant Navy. After his arrival, Conrad made three voyages to the West Indies between 1875 and 1878; During this time, he smuggled guns for the Carlists, who were trying to put Carlos de Bourbon on the throne of Spain. In 1878, Conrad suffered from depression, caused in part by gambling debts and his being forbidden to work on any French ships due to his lying about having the proper permits. He made an unsuccessful attempt at suicide, shooting himself through the shoulder and missing his vital organs. (Biographers differ in their interpretations of this attempt: Some contend that Conrad was depressed about his squandering all his money, while others report that the attempt was a ruse designed to put Conrad out of work and thus escape the grasp of creditors.) Later that year, Conrad boarded an English ship that took him to the eastern port-town of Lowestoft; there, he joined the crew of a ship that made six voyages between Lowestoft and Newcastle. During this time, he learned English. Conrad's determination to succeed as a seaman was impressive: Although he began his career as a common sailor, by 1886 he had sailed to the Asia and was made master of his own ship. He then became a British subject and changed his name to Joseph Conrad (partly to avoid having to return to Poland and serve in the Russian military).

In 1888, Conrad received his first command of the *Otago*, a ship harboring in Bangkok whose master had died. Surprisingly, Conrad hated the day-to-day life of a sailor and never owned a boat after becoming famous; the sea, however, offered Conrad the opportunity to make a living. One of Conrad's most important voyages occurred in 1890, when he sailed a steamboat up the Congo River in central Africa. Conrad was attracted to this region partly because of the adventure he thought it could offer him and (perhaps more importantly) because working in the Congo could earn him some much-needed money. During this voyage, Conrad witnessed incredible barbarity, illness, and inhumanity; his recollections of this trip would eventually become the basis of his most famous work, *Heart of Darkness*. During this time, Conrad was considering turning his seafaring adventures into novels, and he eventually published *Almayer's Folly*, which he had been composing during the early 1890s in 1895. The success of his first novel lured him away from the sea to his new adventures as an English novelist. He settled in England, married Jessie George (in 1896), and began the career for which the world would remember him best.

From Sailor to Author

After the publication of *Almayer's Folly*, Conrad began producing a number of books in rapid succession, many of which featured plots about sailors and travel to explore moral ambiguity and the nature of human identity. *The Nigger of the "Narcissus"* (1897) concerns a tubercular Black sailor whose impending death affects his fellow crewmen in a number of profound ways. *Lord Jim* (1900) examines the effects of a cowardly act and how this act's moral repercussions haunt a man until his death. (Lord Jim's story is told by Marlow, the narrator of *Heart of Darkness*.) In 1902, Conrad published *Heart of Darkness*, a short novel detailing Marlow's journey into the Belgian Congo—and the metaphorical "heart of darkness" of man. All three books were highly regarded in their time and are still widely read and studied today. In 1904, *Nostromo* was published; the complex tale of an imaginary South American republic. The effects of greed and foreign exploitation helped to define Conrad's oblique and sometimes difficult narrative style.

Although he produced a large body of work, Conrad was often a slow writer who felt the pressure of deadlines and the need to keep writing to keep his family financially solvent. His struggles were eased, however, in 1910, when John Quinn, an American lawyer, bought all of Conrad's manuscripts and awarded him a small pension.

Conrad continued writing tales of travel, but also turned his attention to novels of political intrigue. *The Secret Agent* (1907) concerns a group of anarchists who plan to blow up the Greenwich Observatory; *Under Western Eyes* (1911), set in nineteenth-century Czarist Russia, follows the life of a student who betrays his friend—the assassin of a government official—to the authorities. His story "The Secret Sharer" (1912) uses the "Doppelganger theme" (where a man meets his figurative double) to examine what Conrad viewed as the shifting nature of human identity and the essential isolation of all human beings. In 1913, *Chance* was a great success both critically and financially; the novel, like *Heart of Darkness*, explores the ways in which an innocent person (like Marlow) becomes hardened by the horrors that surround her. Other novels marked by these essential Conradian themes include *The Inheritors* (cowritten with Ford Maddox Ford, 1901), *Victory* (1915), and *The Shadow-Line* (1917). Conrad also turned to autobiography: *The Mirror of the Sea* (1906), *A Personal Record* (1912), and *Notes on Life and Letters* (1921). All treat his seafaring days and development as an artist.

Conrad died of heart failure on August 3, 1924. He was buried in Canterbury Cemetery and survived by his wife and sons (Borys and John). Still honored by millions of readers as one of the greatest modern writers, Conrad left behind a large body of work whose nature he defined (in his Preface to *The Nigger of the "Narcissus"*) as "a single-minded attempt to render the highest kind of justice to the visible universe, by bringing to light the truth, manifold and one, underlying its every aspect."

INTRODUCTION TO THE NOVEL

Introduction

Heart of Darkness originally appeared serially in *Blackwood's Magazine* in 1899. It was eventually published as a whole in 1902, as the third work in a volume Conrad titled *Youth*. Since its publication in *Youth*, the novel has fascinated numerous readers and critics, almost all of whom regarded the novel as an important one because of the ways it uses ambiguity and (in Conrad's own words), "foggishness" to dramatize Marlow's perceptions of the horrors he encounters. Critics have regarded *Heart of Darkness* as a work that in several important ways broke many narrative conventions and brought the English novel into the twentieth century.

Notable exceptions who didn't receive the novel well were the British novelist E. M. Forster, who disparaged the very ambiguities that other critics found so interesting, and the African novelist Chinua Achebe, who derided the novel and Conrad as examples of European racism.

Conrad voyaged to the Congo in 1890, when he sailed a steamboat up the Congo River just as Marlow does in the novel. As Conrad writes of the novel in his 1917 Introduction, "*Heart of Darkness* . . . is experience pushed a little (and only very little) beyond the actual facts of the case." Numerous biographical facts find their way into the novel. For example, like Marlow, Conrad had always longed to "follow the sea," the wife of a distant relative (like Marlow's aunt) helped him secure a job with a trading company, the captain who preceded him had been killed by natives in a quarrel (like Fresleven in the novel), and Conrad encountered several men who showed barbaric tendencies similar to the ones exhibited by Kurtz.

What makes *Heart of Darkness* more than an interesting travelogue and shocking account of horrors is the way that it details—in subtle ways—Marlow's gradual understanding of what is happening in this far-off region of the world. Like many Europeans—including his creator—Marlow longed for adventure and devoured accounts such as those offered by Stanley. But once he arrives in the Congo and sees the terrible "work" (as he ironically calls it) taking place, he can no longer hide under the cover of his comfortable civilization. Instead, all the horrors perpetrated by European traders and agents—typified by Kurtz—force him to look into his own soul and find what darkness lies there. In the first half of the novel, Marlow states, "The essentials of this affair lay deep under the surface, beyond my reach"—but by the end of his journey, he will have peeked beneath "the surface" and discovered the inhumanity of which even men such as the once-upstanding Kurtz are capable.

The end of the nineteenth-century brought about one of the most notable examples of imperialism and genocide in modern memory. King Leopold II of Belgium (ruled 1865–1909) possessed an insatiable greed for money, land, and power—and looked to Africa to find them. Like many other Europeans, he was intrigued by reports of Africa made by the famed explorer Henry Morton Stanley (1841-1904), whose books *How I Found Livingstone: Adventures and Discoveries in Central Africa* (1872) and *Through the Dark Continent* (1878) were best-selling accounts of his travels. Through a series of machinations and a deluge of propaganda proclaiming his munificence, Leopold eventually secured the Congo region of Africa as a Belgian colony. On May 20, 1885, Leopold named his new nation the *État Independent du Congo*, or The Congo Free State. This huge area of Africa remained under Belgium control until 1960.

The Congo was a perfect colony for Leopold II for several reasons. First, ivory and rubber were plentiful and could be systematically gathered and shipped to Europe. Second, the only law there was Leopold's: Although he constantly presented himself to his European contemporaries as a philanthropist and humanitarian, Leopold ran the Congo (without ever visiting it) from a distance with an iron hand. Third, labor was plentiful and, more important to Leopold, *free*, because his agents routinely forced the Congolese into slave labor by means of torture or intimidation: Women, for example, were often kidnapped and held until their husbands and sons gathered sufficient quantities of rubber. Forth, there were few operating expenses: Huts and mess-halls were constructed for the agents, and the construction of a railroad system running through the Congo guaranteed that supplies could reach different stations quickly. Finally, the colony was thousands of miles away from sheltered European skies. People could not condemn what they could not see.

Leopold's agents, therefore, comprised a chaotic, unforgiving, and hateful force determined only to make the most money possible by exploiting the natives—often whipping them with a piece of sun-dried hippopotamus hide called a *chicotte*, chopping off their hands and heads, or killing them by dozens at a time. In his recent study of the Congo, *King Leopold's Ghost*, the historian Adam Hochschild estimates that during the period of Leopold's pillage of the Congo, the population dropped by ten million people. Disease, starvation, a low birth rate, and outright murder all combined to turn the Congo into what *Heart of Darkness* later portrayed as a "nightmare." Some observers of the atrocities committed there—such as E. D. Morel and Sir Roger Casement—became noted anti-Leopold activists and launched semi-successful campaigns to end Leopold's rule. Other observers transformed what they saw into art—as did Joseph Conrad when he wrote *Heart of Darkness*.

Leopold's Congo and the people—White and Black—who populated it find their way into the pages of Conrad's novel. The ominous Company that hires Marlow, for example, is a thinly veiled depiction of Leopold's operations in Africa. Leopold's agents become the "faithless pilgrims" looking for riches that Marlow describes once he reaches the Congo, and the chain gang Marlow sees at the Outer Station is a glimpse at the slavery enforced by Leopold's agents. Kurtz, the "first class agent" who commits numerous acts of savagery (including the placing of "rebel" heads upon posts surrounding his hut) is an embodiment of the collective horrors that Conrad witnessed firsthand. As Marlow tells his audience on board the *Nellie*, "In the blinding sunshine of that land I would become acquainted with a flabby, pretending, weak-eyed devil of a rapacious and pitiless folly." The "devil" in this context is the greed that motivated Leopold to continue the systematic ravaging of the Congo and its people for more than twenty years.

A Brief Synopsis

Heart of Darkness begins on the deck of the *Nellie*, a British ship anchored on the coast of the Thames. The anonymous narrator, the Director of Companies, the Accountant, and Marlow sit in silence Marlow begins telling the three men about a time he journeyed in a steamboat up the Congo River. For the rest of the novel (with only minor interruptions), Marlow narrates his tale.

As a young man, Marlow desires to visit Africa and pilot a steamboat on the Congo River. After learning of the Company—a large ivory-trading firm working out of the Congo—Marlow applies for and received a post. He left Europe in a French steamer.

At the Company's Outer Station in the Congo, Marlow witnesses scenes of brutality, chaos, and waste. Marlow speaks with an Accountant, whose spotless dress and uptight demeanor fascinate him. Marlow first learns from the Accountant of Kurtz—a "remarkable" agent working in the interior. Marlow leaves the Outer Station on a 200-mile trek across Africa, and eventually reaches the Company's Central Station, where he learns that the steamboat he is supposed to pilot up the

Congo was wrecked at the bottom of the river. Frustrated, Marlow learns that he has to wait at the Central Station until his boat is repaired.

Marlow then meets the Company's Manager, who told him more about Kurtz. According to the Manager, Kurtz is supposedly ill, and the Manager feigns great concern over Kurtz's health—although Marlow later suspects that the Manager wrecked his steamboat on purpose to keep supplies from getting to Kurtz. Marlow also meets the Brickmaker, a man whose position seems unnecessary, because he doesn't have all the materials for making bricks. After three weeks, a band of traders called The Eldorado Exploring Expedition—led by the Manager's uncle—arrives.

One night, as Marlow is lying on the deck of his salvaged steamboat, he overhears the Manager and his uncle talk about Kurtz. Marlow concludes that the Manager fears that Kurtz is trying to steal his job. His uncle, however, told him to have faith in the power of the jungle to "do away" with Kurtz.

Marlow's boat is finally repaired, and he leaves the Central Station (accompanied by the Manager, some agents, and a crew of cannibals) to bring relief to Kurtz. Approximately fifty miles below Kurtz's Inner Station, they find a hut of reeds, a woodpile, and an English book titled *An Inquiry into Some Points of Seamanship.*

As it crept toward Kurtz, Marlow's steamboat is attacked by a shower of arrows. The Whites fire rifles into the jungle while Marlow tries to navigate the boat. A native helmsman is killed by a large spear and thrown overboard. Assuming that the same natives who are attacking them have already attacked the Inner Station, Marlow feels disappointed now that he will never get the chance to speak to Kurtz.

Marlow reaches the Inner Station and notices Kurtz's building through his telescope—there is no fence, but a series of posts ornamented with "balls" that Marlow later learns were natives' heads. A Russian trader and disciple of Kurtz, called "The Harlequin" by Marlow, approaches the steamboat and tells Marlow that Kurtz is still alive. Marlow learns that the hut they previously saw is the Harlequin's. The Harlequin speaks enthusiastically of Kurtz's wisdom, saying, "This man has enlarged my mind."

Marlow learns from him that the steamboat was attacked because the natives did not want Kurtz to be taken away. Suddenly, Marlow sees a group of native men coming toward him, carrying Kurtz on a stretcher; Kurtz is taken inside a hut, where Marlow approaches him and gives him some letters. Marlow notices that Kurtz is frail, sick, and bald. After leaving the hut, Marlow sees a "wild and gorgeous" native woman approach the steamer; the Harlequin hints to Marlow that the woman is Kurtz's mistress. Marlow then hears Kurtz chiding the Manager from behind a curtain: "Save me!—save the ivory, you mean." The Harlequin, fearing what might happen when Kurtz is taken on board the steamboat, asks Marlow for some tobacco and rifle cartridges; he then leaves in a canoe.

At midnight that same night, Marlow awakens to the sound of a big drum. He inspects Kurtz's cabin, only to discover that he is not there. Marlow runs outside and finds a trail running through the grass—and realizes that Kurtz is escaping by crawling away on all fours. When he comes upon Kurtz, Kurtz warns him to run, but Marlow helps Kurtz to his feet and carried him back to the cabin.

The next day, Marlow, his crew, and Kurtz leave the Inner Station. As they move farther away from the Inner Station, Kurtz's health deteriorates; at one point, the steamboat breaks down and Kurtz gives Marlow a packet of letters and a photograph for safe-keeping, fearing that the Manager will take them. Marlow complies.

One night after the breakdown, Marlow approaches Kurtz, who is lying in the pilothouse on his stretcher "waiting for death." After trying to reassure Kurtz that he is not going to die, Marlow hears Kurtz whisper his final words: "The horror! The horror!" The next day, Kurtz is buried offshore in a muddy hole.

After returning to Europe, Marlow again visits Brussels and finds himself unable to relate to the sheltered Europeans around him. A Company official approaches Marlow and asks for the packet of papers to which Kurtz had entrusted him. Marlow refuses, but he does give the official a copy of Kurtz's report to The Society for the Suppression of Savage Customs with Kurtz's chilling postscript ("Exterminate all the brutes!") torn off. He learns that Kurtz's mother had died after being nursed by Kurtz's "Intended," or fiancée.

Marlow's final duty to Kurtz is to visit his Intended and deliver Kurtz's letters (and her portrait) to her. When he meets her, at her house, she is dressed in mourning and still greatly upset by Kurtz's death. Marlow lets slip that he was with Kurtz when he died, and the Intended asks him to repeat Kurtz's last words Marlow lies to her and says, "The last word he pronounced was—your name." The Intended states that she "knew" Kurtz would have said such a thing, and Marlow leaves, disgusted by his lie yet unable to prevent himself from telling it.

The anonymous narrator on board the *Nellie* then resumes his narrative. The Director of Companies makes an innocuous remark about the tide, and the narrator looks out at the overcast sky and the Thames—which seems to him to lead "into the heart of an immense darkness."

List of Characters

Charlie Marlow a 32 year-old man who has "followed the sea." Marlow's story of his voyage up the Congo River constitutes almost all of Conrad's novel. He pilots the steamboat sent to relieve Kurtz and is shocked by what he sees the European traders have done to the natives.

Kurtz an ivory trader for the Company. Kurtz works out of the Inner Station and is remarkably effective at acquiring ivory. A well-educated European, he is described as a "universal genius" and begins his work in the Congo as part of a virtuous mission. However, while in the jungle, he sets himself up as a god to the natives. By the time Marlow reaches him, he is emaciated and dying.

The Manager Working out of the Central Station, the Manager oversees the Company's activities in the Congo. (He is based on a real person, Camille Delcommune.) The Manager is able to inspires uneasiness in others; Marlow later figures out that he was responsible for the wreck of his steamboat. The Manager fears that Kurtz is trying to steal his job.

The Accountant Also working out of the Central Station, the Accountant somehow manages to wear spotless clothes in the sweltering heat and complains about the groans of a dying man who is brought to his office for fear of being distracted and making clerical errors in the Company's books. He also confides to Marlow some of the Company's shady business practices.

The Brickmaker Although his name suggests the nature of his position, the Brickmaker does not make any bricks because of a shortage of materials. When Marlow meets the Brickmaker at the Central Station, Marlow suspects that he is "pumping" him for information about the Company's plans.

The Harlequin a Russian freelance trader who meets Kurtz in the jungle. He admires Kurtz immensely, telling Marlow, "This man has enlarged my mind."

Kurtz's Native Mistress Kurtz's native mistress. She is very protective of Kurtz and leads a chant on the bank of the river when Kurtz leaves the Inner Station. She dresses in bright colors.

The "Pilgrims" European agents at the Central Station waiting for a chance to be promoted to trading posts, so they can then earn percentages of the ivory they ship back.

The Helmsman a native crewman on Marlow's steamboat. He is killed by a spear during an attack on the boat.

The Doctor When in Brussels, Marlow is examined by the Doctor at the Company's headquarters. He is interested in the effects of the jungle (and the lack of restraint it offers its inhabitants) on European minds.

Marlow's Aunt Using her influence with the wife of a high Company official, she helps Marlow get his post as a steamboat pilot for the Company.

Kurtz's Intended A demure and mourning young woman; Marlow visits her after he returns to Europe and lies to her about her fiancée's last words. She is dressed in black.

The Narrator An unnamed man on board the *Nellie* who relates Marlow's story to the reader.

Character Map

Heart of Darkness

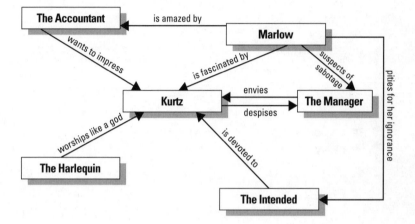

The Congo in 1900

CRITICAL COMMENTARIES

Part 1

Summary

Heart of Darkness begins on board the *Nellie*, a small ship moored on the Thames River in London. After describing the river and its slow-moving traffic, the unnamed narrator offers short descriptions of London's history to his companions who, with him, lazily lounge on the deck, waiting for the tide to turn. With him are the Director of Companies (their Captain), a lawyer, an accountant, and Marlow, the novel's protagonist. As the sun sets, the four men become contemplative and brooding; eventually, Marlow breaks the spell of silence by beginning his tale about his voyage to the Congo.

The other men remain silent while Marlow collects his ideas, after which he begins the story proper. The remainder of the novel becomes (with a few exceptions) the narrator's report of what Marlow tells him and the others on board the *Nellie*. Conrad's novel is thus a *frame tale*, or story-within-a-story.

As a boy, Marlow was fascinated by maps and yearned to become a seaman or explorer who could visit the most remote parts of the earth. As a young man, Marlow spent approximately six years sailing in the Pacific before returning to London—where he then saw, in a shop window, a map of Africa and the Congo River. Recalling the news of a Continental trading Company operating in the Congo, Marlow became determined to pilot a steamboat to find adventure in Africa. He asked his aunt, who knew the wife of a Company official to assist him in getting a job as a pilot; she happily complied.

Marlow hurried across the English Channel to sign his contracts at the Company's headquarters in Brussels. Passing through an office with two women who are knitting, Marlow spoke with the Company's director for less than a minute; after being dismissed, he was asked to sign a number of papers in which he promised not to divulge any trade secrets. Marlow finally reached the mouth of the Congo. Finding passage on a little sea-bound steamer to take him where his steamboat awaited him, Marlow spoke with its Swedish captain about the Company and the effects of the jungle on Europeans. The Swede then told Marlow a short yet ominous story about a man he took upriver who hanged himself on the road. Shocked, Marlow asked why, only to be told that perhaps the "sun" or the "country" were too much for him. Eventually, they reached the Company's Outer Station, which amounted to three wooden buildings on the side of a rocky slope. Out of this station was shipped the Company's most important and lucrative commodity: ivory.

Marlow spent the next ten days waiting for the caravan to conduct him to the Central Station (and his steamboat), during which time he saw more of the Accountant. On some days, Marlow would sit in his office, trying to avoid the giant "stabbing" flies. When a stretcher with a sick European was put in the office temporarily, the Accountant became annoyed with his groans, complaining that they distracted him and increased the chances for clerical errors. Noting Marlow's ultimate destination in the interior region of the Congo, the Accountant hinted that Marlow would "no doubt meet Mr. Kurtz," a Company agent in charge of an incredibly lucrative ivory-post deep in the interior. The Accountant described Kurtz as a "first class agent" and "remarkable person" whose station brought in more ivory than all the other stations combined. He asked Marlow to tell Kurtz that everything at the Outer Station was satisfactory and then hinted that Kurtz was being groomed for a high position in the Company's Administration.

The day after this conversation, Marlow left the Outer Station with a caravan of sixty men for a two hundred-mile "tramp" to the Central Station. (The men were native porters who carried the equipment, food and water.) Marlow saw innumerable paths cut through the jungle and a number of abandoned villages along the way. He saw a drunken White man, who claimed to be looking after the "upkeep" of a road, and the body of a native who was shot in the head. Marlow's one White companion was an overweight man who kept fainting due to the heat. Eventually, he had to be carried in a hammock, and when the hammock skinned his nose and was dropped by the natives, he demanded that Marlow do something to punish them. Marlow did nothing except press onward until they reached the Central Station, where an "excitable chap" informed him that his steamboat was at the bottom of the river; two days earlier, the bottom of the boat had been torn off when some "volunteer skipper" piloted it upriver to have it ready for Marlow's arrival.

Marlow was therefore forced to spend time at the Central Station. As he did with the Outer Station, he relates to his audience on the *Nellie* his impressions of the place. Marlow met a Brickmaker (although

Marlow did not see a brick anywhere) who pressed him for information about the Company's activities in Europe. When Marlow confessed to knowing nothing about the secret intrigues of the Company, the Brickmaker assumed he was lying and became annoyed.

At this point, Marlow breaks off his narrative, explaining to the men on the *Nellie* that he finds it difficult to convey the dream-like quality of his African experiences.

Marlow resumes his tale by continuing the description of his talk with the Brickmaker, who complained to Marlow that he could never find the necessary materials needed to make any bricks. Marlow told of how he needed rivets to repair his steamboat, but none arrived in any of the caravans.

After his conversation with the Brickmaker, Marlow told his mechanic (a boilermaker) that their rivets would be arriving shortly. (Marlow assumed that because the Brickmaker was eager to please him because he assumed Marlow had important friends, he would get him the necessary rivets.) Like the Brickmaker, the mechanic assumed that Marlow had great influence in Europe. However, the rivets did not arrive—instead, a number of white men riding donkeys (and followed by a number of natives) burst into the Central Station. Marlow learned that these men called themselves the Eldorado Exploring Expedition and that they had arrived in search of treasure. The Manager's uncle was the leader of the Expedition, and Marlow saw him and his nephew conspiring on many occasions. At times, Marlow would hear Kurtz's name mentioned and become mildly curious, but he felt a strong desire to repair his steamship and begin his job as a pilot.

Commentary

Heart of Darkness is best known as the story of Marlow's journey to Africa, which, in part, it is. However, the novel is also the story of a man on board a London ship who *listens* to Marlow's story as well. This "story-within-a-story" form is called a *frame tale*. (The significance of the framing device is discussed in the Critical Essays section.)

Exploring man's inhumanity toward other men and raising some troubling questions about the impulse toward imperialism, *Heart of Darkness* is also an adventure story where (such as many others) the young hero embarks on a journey, and in the process, learns about himself. Marlow begins his narrative as a rough-and-ready young man searching for adventure. Unlike those of Europe, the maps of Africa still contained some "blank spaces" that Marlow yearned to explore; his likening the Congo River to a snake suggests the mesmeric powers of Africa. However, the serpent is also a well-known symbol of evil and temptation, harkening back to the Book of Genesis in the Old Testament. Thus, Conrad's comparing the river to a snake also suggests the danger Marlow will find in Africa and the temptations to which Kurtz succumbs when he sets himself up as a god to the natives. Despite the uncertainty of what lay there, Marlow had to go.

Literary Device

However, before Marlow even sets foot on the African shore, Conrad begins to alert the reader to the terrible power of the African jungle. Marlow learns that a piloting position has become open because a chief's son has killed one of the Company's pilots over two black hens. Fresleven, the dead pilot, was thought by all to be "the kindliest, gentlest creature that ever walked on two legs," but Conrad hints that *something* caused him to shed his self-control (as a snake sheds its skin) and attack the chief of a village. (This *something*, being the effects of "the jungle" on uninitiated Europeans, becomes more and more pronounced to Marlow and the reader as the novel progresses.) Marlow eventually sees Fresleven's remains on the ground with grass growing up through the bones. The image suggests that Africa itself has won a battle against Fresleven and all he represents. The earth reclaimed him as its own, and Nature has triumphed over civilization. This is the first lesson Marlow learns about the futility of the Company's agents' attempts to remain "civilized" in the jungle, which releases instinctual and primitive drives within them that they did not ever think they possessed.

Theme

When Marlow visits Brussels to get his appointment, he describes the city as a "whited sepulcher"—a Biblical phrase referring to a hypocrite or person who employs a façade of goodness to mask his or her true malignancy. The Company, like its headquarters, is a similar "whited sepulcher," proclaiming its duty to bring "civilization" and "light" to Africa in the name of Christian charity, but really raping the land and its people in the name of profit and the lust for power. Marlow's aunt, who talks to him about "weaning those ignorant millions from their horrid ways" serves as an example of how deeply the Company's propaganda has been ingrained into the minds of Europeans. Uncomfortable with his aunt's ideas, Marlow suggests that the Company is simply "run for profit"; before he sees *how* these profits are acquired, he is blissfully unaware of the Company's depravity. Marlow dwells in the realm of wishful thinking, wanting to believe that the Company has no imperialistic impulses and is simply an economic enterprise, much like the ones to which he is accustomed as a European.

Literary Device

The first glimpse Marlow and the reader have of the Company's headquarters hints at the organization's sinister, evil, and conspiratorial atmosphere. First, Marlow "slipped through one of the cracks" to enter the building, implying that the Company is figuratively "closed" in terms of what it allows the public to learn about its operations.

Second, the two women knitting black wool suggest the Fates of Greek mythology; like these goddesses, the Company is "knitting" the destiny of the Africans, represented by the black wool. The Company, therefore, plays God with the lives of the Africans, deciding who in the Congo will live or die.

Third, Marlow is led into a dimly lit office—the lighting reflects the "shady" and ambiguous morals of the Company. He only speaks with the Company's President for forty-five seconds, suggesting that the Company views Marlow—and people like him—as expendable.

Fourth, Marlow is asked to sign "some document" that ostensibly contracts him to not reveal "any trade secrets," but figuratively suggests the selling of his soul to the Devil. (As the Manager of the Central Station will later remark about Africa, "Men who come out here should have no entrails.") As the Devil seeks human souls to overthrow eventually God in Heaven, the Company is metaphorically seeking to acquire the souls of as many Europeans as possible to make greater profits.

Fifth, when Marlow is examined by the Company's Doctor, he learns that many Europeans who venture to Africa become mad: When the Doctor begins measuring Marlow's skull, the reader infers Conrad's point that European "science" and "technology" (even with a science as ludicrous as phrenology) are no match for the power if the jungle. When "civilized" Europeans go to Africa, the restraints placed upon them by European society begin to vanish, resulting in the kind of behavior previously seen in Fresleven. Later in the novel, when his anger begins to grow after finding all of his gear damaged by the porters, Marlow ironically remarks, "I felt I was becoming scientifically interesting."

Also worth noting is the abundance of white and dark images in these opening pages of Marlow's narrative. The Congo is described as a "*white* patch" on a map, Fresleven was killed in a scuffle over two *black* hens, Brussels is a "*whited* sepulcher," the two women knit *black* wool and the old one wears a "starched *white* affair," the President's secretary has *white* hair, and the Doctor has black *ink-stains* on his sleeves. Many critics have commented (sometimes inconclusively) on Conrad's use of white and black imagery; generally, one should note how the *combination* of white and black images suggests several of the novel's ideas:

The Company claims to be a means by which (as Marlow's aunt calls them), "emissaries of light" can bring civilization to the "darkness" of Africa, which is done by denoting Brussels as white and the Congo as white.

The white men in the novel (particularly Marlow and Kurtz) will be greatly influenced by their experiences with the Africans.

Although the Company professes to be a force of "white" moral righteousness, it is actually "spotted" with "black" spots of sin and inhumanity, and the corpses of the Black natives that are found throughout the Congo.

In short, the Company may *appear* to be "white" and pure, but it is actually quite the opposite, as denoted by the accountant and his white shirt.

Some critics, have claimed that Conrad's use of "darkness" to represent evil suggests the racist assumptions of the novel; others argue that the "white" characters in the book are actually more "black" than the natives they slaughter and that Conrad's imagery stresses the hypocrisy of the Company and its "white" employees. Regardless of this critical dispute, a reader should note that Conrad toys with white and black imagery throughout the course of the novel, and of course, in its very title.

Character Insight

Marlow feels like "an imposter" when he leaves the Company's headquarters, because he has joined the ranks of an outfit whose assumptions about Africa and European activity there sharply contrast with his own. Marlow has no imperialistic impulses and only seeks adventure—but he is beginning to see the Company for what it truly is. Thus, Marlow's growing perception of the moral decay around him becomes one of the major issues of the novel.

Like the Company headquarters, Africa itself is initially portrayed as an enchanting and intriguing place. The continent is described as unfinished and "still in the making," possessing an air that beguiles Europeans to "Come and find out" if they can survive there.

This portrayal of Africa as an untouched paradise, however, is quickly countered by Marlow's description. He notices a French man-of-war firing its guns into the bush; the "pop" made by its guns highlights the Company's ineffectual attempts to subdue the continent. Similarly, Marlow notices a boiler lying in the grass, an unused railway car resembling "the carcass of some animal," a series of explosions that do nothing to change the rock they are attempting to remove, an "artificial hole" the purpose of which he cannot discern, and a ravine filled with broken drainage pipes. Stunned by these images of chaos, Marlow remarks, "The work was going on. The work!" Clearly, these signs of waste and ineptitude are not what Marlow expected to see upon his arrival; these discarded machines symbolize the complete disregard of the Company for making any real progress in the Congo, as well as the disorganization that marks its day-to-day operations.

Even more disturbing to Marlow is the "grove of death": a shady spot where some of the natives—like the machinery mentioned previously—are dying without anyone seeming to notice or care. Calling them "nothing but black shadows of disease and starvation" and "bundles of acute angles," Marlow attempts to show some charity by offering one of them a biscuit; the dying native, however, can only grasp it in his hand, too weak to even bring it to his mouth. Marlow notices that this man has "a bit of white worsted" tied around his neck and puzzles over its meaning, but the reader can see that the wool is symbolic of the Company's "collaring" the natives and treating them like animals. Disturbed, Marlow leaves the grove to soothe his shaken mind. Rather than confront the horror head-on, he retreats; later he will not have this luxury.

Marlow moves from the natives to a European: the Company's chief accountant, who suggests the immense amount of money that the Company is making from its campaign of terror and whose dress is impeccable. Again the reader sees the Company's attempts to array itself in colors and façades of purity. Marlow calls the Accountant a "miracle" because of his ability to keep up a dignified European appearance amidst the sweltering and muddy jungle. (He even has a penholder behind his ear.) Completely and willingly oblivious to the horrors around him, the Accountant cares only for figures and his own importance: When a sick agent is temporarily placed in his hut, the Accountant complains. He also tells Marlow, "When one has got to make correct entries, one comes to hate those savages—hate them to the death." To the Company, as embodied in the Accountant, profits take precedence over human life and the bottom line is more important than any higher law of humanity.

Marlow's two hundred-mile hike to the Central Station reinforces the Company's lack of organization and brutality. Passing through deserted and razed villages, his perception of the Company becomes sharper. His journey ends at the Central Station, where Marlow spends the remainder of Part 1. Like the Company's European headquarters and the Outer Station, this place reeks of waste, inhumanity, and death. Earlier in the novel, Marlow states that he would, in time, "become acquainted with a flabby, pretending, weak-eyed devil of a rapacious and pitiless folly"—now, at the Central Station, he remarks, "the first glance of the place was enough to let you see the flabby devil was running that show." No longer the enthusiastic sailor, Marlow grows increasingly suspicious and judgmental of what he sees. The fact that he learns, upon his arrival, that his steamboat is at the bottom of the river only increases his ire and suspicion.

A noteworthy segment of Part 1 concerns Kurtz's painting, which Marlow sees hanging in the Brickmaker's room. The painting depicts a woman, blindfolded, carrying a lighted torch. Clearly, this woman reminds one of the usual personification of justice, while the torch suggests the Company bringing the "light" of civilization into the "Dark Continent." (Recall Marlow's aunt and her hope that Marlow will help those "ignorant" savages become more civilized.) The woman in the painting also symbolizes the Company, which willingly blindfolds itself to the horrors it perpetuates in the name of profit; it also recalls the Company's ineptitude and the ways in which it "blindly" stumbles through Africa.

This painting also symbolizes its creator. Like the blindfolded woman, Kurtz once yearned to bring the "light" of civilization and progress to the "dark" continent. (This explains the torch coming out of the darkness.) At the end of his life, however, Kurtz changes his position, most markedly apparent when Marlow reads a handwritten line in one of Kurtz's reports urging, "Exterminate all the brutes!" Thus, according to the painting, Europe puts on a show of bringing "light"— but this light ultimately reveals a "sinister" appearance, which marks the woman's face. Here, Conrad foreshadows what Kurtz will be like when Marlow meets him: a man who once held high ideals about bringing "justice" and "light" to the Congo, but who became "sinister" once he arrived there.

One of Conrad's personifications of the "flabby" (because it has "devoured" Africa), "pretending" (because it masquerades its avarice in the name of enlightenment), and "weak-eyed" (because it refuses to "see" the effects of its work) Company is the Manager. He has no education, is a "common trader," inspires "neither fear nor love," creates "uneasiness" in all who meet him, and lacks any "genius for organizing." All Marlow is able to conclude is that he "was never ill" and is able to keep the supply of ivory flowing to European ports. Marlow's growing perceptions soon allow him to understand that the Company possesses "not an atom of foresight or of serious intention" and that "To tear treasure out of the bowels of the land was their desire, with no more moral purpose at the back of it than there is in burglars breaking into a safe."

At this point, Conrad increases the amount of rumors and half-truths that Marlow (and the reader) begins to hear about "the man who is so indissolubly connected" with Marlow's journey: Kurtz. As *Heart of Darkness* progresses, Conrad's emphasis shifts from Marlow's desire to explore the "snake" of the Congo to his longing to meet this shadowy figure. Kurtz is first mentioned by the Accountant, who calls him "a first-class agent" and "a remarkable person" who "sends in as much ivory as the others put together." The Manager, however, speaks of Kurtz in more ambiguous terms.

In spite of his claims of concern for Kurtz, the Manager is actually sabotaging Kurtz and doing everything in his power to ensure that he will die at the Inner Station. His motive? Professional jealousy. Marlow notices "an air of plotting" at the station and later overhears the Manager speaking to his uncle (the leader of the Eldorado Exploring Expedition), from which he learns the following things:

The Manager, against his will, was forced to send Kurtz to the interior of the jungle: "Am I the Manager—or am I not?" he asks.

Kurtz *asked* the administration to send him there with the idea of "showing what he could do."

The Manager fears that Kurtz "has the council by the nose" and has requested a position in the interior because he wants the Manager's job: "Conceive you—that ass! And he wants to be Manager!"

Thus, the Manager is nervous when talking to Marlow because he does not know who Marlow really is or if he has any powerful connections in Europe. When he replies, "That ought to do the affair," he means that three months without any relief should be long enough to ensure Kurtz's death. "Trust to this," his uncle says as he gestures to the jungle, and this is just what the Manager is doing: "Trusting" that (as his uncle also says) "the climate may do away with this difficulty" for him. Only later does Marlow realize that the Manager was responsible for his steamboat's "accident": He could not get any rivets because the Manager made sure that their delivery to Marlow was delayed as long as possible without arousing Marlow's suspicions. (When Marlow's steamboat gets close to Kurtz in Part 2, the Manager tells Marlow to wait until the next morning before pressing on, to delay their arrival even more than he already has.) Even as Marlow felt he was being entered into a giant conspiracy upon accepting his post in Europe, he has unwittingly stumbled upon one in the Congo.

The brickmaker who tries to wrangle information out of Marlow about Kurtz adds to the conspiratorial air of the Central Station. From his conversation with Marlow, the reader learns that Kurtz has disrupted the brickmaker's plans to become assistant-manager. The brickmaker also reflects the Company's disorganization, for he makes no bricks at all; he also reflects the Company's avarice, for he wants to advance in rank without completing any actual work.

While the plot concerning Marlow's steamboat and rivets adds to Conrad's overall air of conspiracy, it also metaphorically enriches the novel as a whole. Rivets *hold things together*, and Conrad uses the rivets as symbols of the ways in which the Company, the Manager, Marlow, Kurtz, and Kurtz's fiancée (his Intended) attempt to "hold together" their beliefs and ideas. These ideological "rivets" are seen in numerous ways. For example, the Company wants to keep its operations running without criticism, inquiry or restraint; Marlow wants to believe his own naïve ideas about Africa; Kurtz wants to remain king of his private empire and disregard his "civilized" self; and the Intended wants to believe that Kurtz was a great man with a "generous mind" and "noble heart." Each character has his or her own "rivet," from the Company's implied belief that it is "civilizing" the Africans to the Intended's acceptance of Marlow's lie about Kurtz. *Heart of Darkness* is an oftentimes disturbing book because Conrad's suggestion that all of these "rivets" are simply lies—ideas, beliefs and assumptions used to excuse shameless profiteering (as with the Company) or sustain a false image of a loved one (as with the Intended). Only Marlow and Kurtz see that these metaphorical "rivets" are faulty: Marlow when he witnesses firsthand the atrocities perpetuated by the Company and Kurtz when he whispers,

"The horror! The horror!" on his deathbed. Marlow's naïve belief that the Company was run only for profit and Kurtz's belief that he could escape his own "civilized" morality are both shown to be "rivets" that simply could not hold.

The final symbol found in Part 1 is the Eldorado Exploring Expedition, run by the Manager's uncle. This fictional expedition is based on an actual one: The Katanga Expedition (1890-92). The fact that the Manager's uncle leads the expedition suggests that it is another example of White traders scrambling for riches in the Congo. Marlow dismisses them as "buccaneers" who do not even make a pretense of coming to Africa for anything other than treasure.

Glossary

(Here and in the following sections, difficult words and phrases, as well as allusions and historical references, are explained.)

Cruising yawl a small, two-masted sailing vessel.

Gravesend a seaport on the Thames River in southwest England.

the greatest town on earth London.

Sir Francis Drake (c. 1540-96) English admiral and buccaneer: 1st Englishman to sail around the world.

Sir John Franklin (1786-1847) English Arctic explorer.

the Golden Hind a ship sailed by the English navigator Sir Francis Drake (c. 1540-96) during the reign of Elizabeth I.

the Erebus and Terror In 1845, the English Arctic explorer Sir John Franklin led a voyage in the ships *Erebus* and *Terror* in search of the Northwest Passage; the ships were stuck in ice from April 1846 to September 1848.

They had sailed from Deptford, from Greenwich, from Erith Deptford, Greenwich, and Erith are three ports between London and Gravesend.

men on 'Change Men working in a place where merchants meet to do business; exchange.

trireme an ancient Greek or Roman galley, usually a warship, with three banks of oars on each side.

Gauls the Celtic-speaking people dwelling in the ancient region of Western Europe consisting of what is now mainly France & Belgium: after 5th century B.C.

Falerian wine wine made in a district of Campania, Italy.

a mighty big river the Congo River in Africa.

Fleet Street an old street in central London, where several newspaper and printing offices are located; the term "Fleet Street" has come to refer to the London press.

whited sepulchre in the Bible, a phrase used to describe a hypocrite. The relevant allusion in Matthew is "beautiful to look at on the outside, but inside full of filth and dead men's bones." Brussels. The hypocrisy alluded to is that King Leopold's brutal colonial empire was run from this beautiful, seemingly civilized, city.

Ave! Old knitter of black wool. Morituri te salutant. Literally, "Hail! Those who are about to die salute you"; a salute of the gladiators in ancient Rome to whomever was hosting their tournaments. Here, Marlow is ironically comparing the knitters to Roman emperors.

Plato (c. 427- c.347 B.C.) Greek philosopher.

alienist an old term for a psychiatrist.

Du calme, du calme. Adieu. French: "Stay calm, stay calm. Goodbye."

Zanzibaris natives of Zanzibar, an island off the E coast of Africa: 640 sq. mi. (1,657 sq. km).

sixteen stone 224 pounds; a stone is a British unit of weight equal to 14 pounds (6.36 kilograms).

assegais slender spears or javelins with iron tips, used in southern Africa.

serviette a table napkin.

Ichthyosaurus a prehistoric reptile with four paddle-like flippers.

Part 2

Summary

One evening Marlow eavesdropped on the Manager and his uncle as they discussed Kurtz. Marlow learned that Kurtz asked the Company's Administration to send him into the jungle to show how much ivory he could acquire, and that he sent his assistant back to the Manager because he found him inadequate for the work. Marlow further learned that there were "strange rumours" circulating about Kurtz's behavior. The Manager insinuated that he hoped Kurtz would die in the jungle. A few days later, the Eldorado Expedition entered the jungle; they had no news except that all the donkeys were dead. His steamboat repaired, Marlow began his voyage to the Inner Station, accompanied by the Manager, the other agents whom Marlow calls "pilgrims," and 20 natives (who were also cannibals).

About fifty miles below the Inner Station, the steamboat came across a hut of reeds; near the hut were the remnants of a flag and a neatly stacked woodpile. Near the woodpile, written on a board, were the words, "Wood for you. Hurry up. Approach cautiously." Inside the hut, Marlow found evidence of a White tenant: a rudely formed table, a heap of rubbish, and a book about seamanship with some sort of code written in the margins. The natives took the wood (to power the steamboat) and Marlow slipped the book in his pocket.

When they were about a mile and a half below the Inner Station, unseen, silent natives who fired small arrows attacked the steamboat. The pilgrims fired their guns into the bush while the attack continued, the helmsman soon being killed by a spear.

Finally, Marlow reached the Inner Station. He first saw a "long, decaying building" with a number of posts around it; each post was topped with a "round curved ball." (Later, Marlow discovered that the building was Kurtz's quarters and that the "balls" were human heads.) A white man met them at the shore and reminded Marlow of a harlequin; he informed them that Kurtz was still alive. The Harlequin then explained that the natives attacked Marlow's steamboat because they did not want anyone to take Kurtz away from them.

Commentary

Style & Language

Part 2 of *Heart of Darkness* offers the reader some of Conrad's most dense passages. Sentences such as, "It was the stillness of an implacable force brooding over an inscrutable intention" may seem confusing, but the difficulty here instead is Marlow's, because much of *Heart of Darkness* concerns how its protagonist struggles to articulate what traveling through the jungle is *like*. Marlow explains to his companions on the *Nellie* that they cannot fully grasp the whole truth of what he saw, because they live in the modern, "civilized" world with "a butcher round one corner, a policeman round another, excellent appetites, and temperature normal." Marlow's point here is that language sometimes fails to wholly convey the wonders and horrors of his experience; his remark, "This is the worst of trying to tell," suggests his difficulty in relating to his companions the full emotional, spiritual, and political impact that his journey had on him. His companions will not be able to fully understand him because they live with the "solid pavement" of Europe under their feet. This idea that Marlow's *telling* of the story is a major part of the story itself is suggested by the anonymous narrator who, at the beginning of the novel, explains that, for Marlow, "the meaning of an episode was not inside like a kernel but outside, enveloping the tale which brought it out only as a glow brings out a haze." In other words, *Heart of Darkness* is as much the story of a man coming face-to-face with a number of political, moral, and spiritual horrors as much as it is one of that same man's search for language adequate enough to convey them. Hence, the novel is by turns both striking and obtuse, both concrete and abstract, both detailed and ambiguous.

Note that Marlow pauses at one point in Part 2 and the flow of his story is broken by the frame narrator's words. This reminds the reader of the fact that Marlow is *telling* his story instead of living through it—and that what he knows about the story's issues as a whole will affect the ways he relates it to the men on the *Nellie*. There are essentially two Marlows: The one who lived through the experience and the one who looks back on it. Marlow's digression about Kurtz, therefore, allows the reader to eventually meet Kurtz with Marlow's opinions of him in mind.

In Part 1, Marlow calls the forest "primeval" and jokes that he expected to see an "ichthyosaurus" while voyaging through it. Throughout Part 2, Marlow's description of the jungle is marked by an increased emphasis on what he sees as its prehistoric nature. "Going back to that jungle was like traveling back to the earliest beginnings of the world," he states, and subsequent passages reinforce this impression. For example, he calls himself and his crew "wanderers on a prehistoric earth" and the natives examples of "prehistoric man." Marlow also stresses the unreality of the jungle that can make one "bewitched" and cut off from everything one had ever known. The tiny steamboat, "clinging to the skirts of the unknown," causes Marlow to feel small and lost.

Theme

This attitude may seem patronizing—as if Marlow implies that Africa is unfinished and is ages behind Europe in terms of civilization. However, much of Conrad's novel is a critique of civilization and those who want (like Kurtz) to bring its "light" into the heart of "darkness." Similarly, modern readers may regard where Marlow discusses his connections to the natives as Eurocentric or even racist.

To a European in 1899, the thought of one's kinship with "savages" may, indeed, seem "ugly"—but Marlow's point here is that only someone with the necessary courage could see that the differences between "enlightened" Europe and the "prehistoric" Congo are superficial ones. This is one of the things that Marlow learns from Kurtz and that is stressed when, during the attack on the steamboat, Marlow sees "a face amongst the leaves on the level with my own, looking at me very fierce and steady." The Company may bring no real "light" to Africa, but Marlow is increasingly "enlightened" about his own humanity.

Still, Marlow is not yet the Buddha preaching in European clothes he will become on board the *Nellie*. Instead, he concentrates on steering the steamboat and avoiding snags to save his mind from considering all of these philosophical and political implications. Focusing on "work" instead of deeper moral concerns is what saves Marlow's sanity— and by extension, allows the Company to ravage the Congo without a moment's pause. Piloting is the "rivet" that holds together Marlow as he comes closer to Kurtz, who will upset all of Marlow's "surface-truths" (as he calls them) and force him to consider all the ugliness of which Marlow has been a part.

Marlow does speak well of the cannibals on board his steamboat, for they possess a quality that Marlow sees less and less during his time in Company-controlled Africa: restraint. Although these men "still belonged to the beginnings of time," they never attack their White superiors—which would have been an easy feat for them. Marlow argues that "the devilry of lingering starvation" is the most impossible force to defeat, because it outweighs any "superstitions, beliefs, and what you may call principles." Unlike the Company (and its greatest prodigy, Kurtz), the "savage" Africans show a humane and honorable restraint that their "superiors" obviously lack, as seen in their insatiable hunger for ivory and the brutal means by which they acquire it.

As the jungle grows more frightening and mysterious, Marlow struggles to keep himself calm and "European." His joy in finding the Harlequin's book reflects his longing for a sign of his previous world as he trudges through this new one. Despite the fact that the book itself (*An Inquiry into Some Points of Seamanship*) looks "dreary reading enough," Marlow is excited by its very existence as "something unmistakably real." The book's subject matter and author (a "Master in His Majesty's Navy"), while dry, are evidence of "science" and "an honest concern for the right way of going to work." When he is summoned to the steamboat, Marlow confesses that putting down the book is like "tearing myself away from the shelter of an old and solid friendship"; the "friendship" of which Marlow speaks is his long one with Europe, which has always kept him "sheltered" from the truth of his kinship with "savagery."

The death of the helmsman is another scene where Marlow attempts to make the reality of his situation "fade." After finding that the helmsman has been killed in the attack, Marlow is "morbidly anxious" to change his shoes and socks.

Literary
Device

In addition to intensifying the reader's understanding of Marlow's impending epiphany, Part 2 contains a digression where he abandons his narrative and speaks of Kurtz in a general sense. Unlike the cannibals, Kurtz possessed a ravenous hunger: "You should have heard him say . . . 'My Intended, my ivory, my station, my river, my—' everything." His bald head suggested the ivory that he had spent so much effort in securing. His "nerves went wrong" and he participated in "unspeakable rites." He "had taken a high seat among the devils of the land" and Marlow found it impossible to know "how many powers of darkness had claimed him for their own." However, what is more striking than these elusive hints at barbarity is Marlow's short yet important *defense* of Kurtz: "All Europe contributed to the making of Kurtz." Literally, Marlow is speaking of Kurtz's ancestry—but metaphorically, Marlow implies that the horrors he saw in Africa cannot all be blamed on one man. More importantly, Kurtz is not an isolated figure— all of Europe has produced him, and the power, hunger, and evil he embodies. The appearance of the Harlequin (like Kurtz's jester) at this point emphasizes the charisma and power of the demagogue and prepares the reader—like the previously discussed digression—for the entrance of Kurtz in Part 3.

Glossary

Winchesters a type of magazine rifle, first made in the 1860s.

sounding-pole a pole used to determine the depth of a body of water.

scow a large, flat-bottomed boat with square ends, used for carrying coal, sand, and so on and often towed by a tug.

Martini-Henry a military rifle.

fusillade a simultaneous or rapid and continuous discharge of many firearms.

Part 3

Summary

The Harlequin told Marlow that he had spent many nights listening to Kurtz speak about a variety of subjects. Marlow further learned that Kurtz was prone to wandering into the jungle with his band of native followers on ivory raids. While listening to the Harlequin, Marlow looked through his binoculars at Kurtz's quarters and discovered that the round knobs he previously saw on the posts bordering the house were the heads of native "rebels," turned inward to face Kurtz as he sat inside. Suddenly, Marlow saw a group of natives appear from a corner of the house, bearing Kurtz on a stretcher. Fearing an attack, Marlow, the Harlequin, and everyone on the steamboat stood still—until Marlow saw Kurtz's emaciated arm emerge from the stretcher and order his army to leave. The Manager and other agents laid Kurtz in his bed and delivered his belated pieces of mail.

Marlow left Kurtz's room and saw, on the bank of the river, Kurtz's African mistress, who captivated Marlow with her pride, stature, and appearance. She boarded the steamboat for a minute without speaking, lifted her arms, and then vanished into the bush. Marlow then heard Kurtz speaking derisively to the Manager from inside his room. Trying to appear nonplussed, the Manager came out of the room and told Marlow that, while Kurtz had amassed a remarkable quantity of ivory, he was low and that his ivory district would have to be closed because his method was unsound. Fearful of the Manager's intentions, the Harlequin told Marlow his suspicion that Kurtz's White rescuers were actually trying to hurt him. Recalling the overheard conversation between the Manager and his uncle, Marlow told the Harlequin that he was correct. The Harlequin then revealed that Kurtz had ordered the attack on the steamboat because "he hated the idea of being taken away." The Harlequin asked Marlow to guard Kurtz's reputation once he arrived in Europe, asked him for some rifle cartridges and shoes, and then left the Inner Station.

Shortly after midnight, Marlow awoke to the sounds of a drumbeat and natives reciting incantations. After hearing a "burst of yells," Marlow entered Kurtz's room and found he had escaped. He found Kurtz crawling through the grass and finally approached him. At first, Kurtz told Marlow to run and hide himself—but he then began telling Marlow that he had "immense plans" that were ruined by the Manager. Marlow listened, hoping that Kurtz would make no noise or give no sign for his men to attack. Finally, Marlow led Kurtz back to his room.

They left the Inner Station the next day. As they floated downstream, three natives covered in bright red earth shouted some form of spell; they next saw Kurtz's native mistress run to the riverbank and begin shouting something that the rest of Kurtz's 1,000 followers began repeating. The Whites on the steamboat began pointing their rifles at the shore; to avoid a massacre, Marlow began blowing the whistle to scare the natives away. Many of them ran, but the "wild woman" did not. The Whites on deck then opened fire on Kurtz's followers.

As they made their way to the sea (and Europe), Kurtz continued to talk of his ideas, plans, station, and career. Kurtz gave Marlow a packet of papers and a photograph and asked him to keep it for him, out of reach of the Manager. One evening, after repairing the engine, Marlow entered Kurtz's room and heard him whisper his final words: "The horror! The horror!" Marlow entered the mess-room and refused to meet the inquiring eyes of the Manager. Eventually, the Manager's servant boy peeked into the mess-room and announced, in a contemptuous voice, "Mistah Kurtz—he dead." Kurtz was buried in the jungle the next day. Stricken by Kurtz's death, Marlow almost considered suicide, and the remainder of his journey back to Europe is omitted from his narrative.

Back in Brussels, Marlow's aunt tried to nurse him back to health. An unnamed representative of the Company then visited Marlow and wanted the papers that Kurtz had given to Marlow. As he did when pressed by the Manager on their voyage home, Marlow refused. He eventually gave the man the copy of Kurtz's report on "The Suppression of Savage Customs," but with the postscript ("Exterminate all the brutes!") torn off. Marlow then met Kurtz's cousin, who told Marlow that Kurtz was a great musician and a "universal genius." Marlow gave him some unimportant family letters from the packet. A journalist then accosted Marlow, eager for information about Kurtz. As they talked, the journalist told Marlow that Kurtz could have been a great politician for any party, because he had the charisma and voice to "electrify" large meetings. Marlow gave him Kurtz's report on "Savage Customs" and the journalist said he would print it.

Marlow thought it necessary to visit Kurtz's Intended—his fiancée, whose photograph Kurtz had given Marlow on the voyage home. Marlow waited for her in her drawing room until she entered, dressed in mourning. She immediately struck Marlow as trustworthy, sincere, and innocent. As she told Marlow that no one knew Kurtz as well as she, he struggled to maintain his composure, because he did not want to reveal to her what Kurtz actually became during his time in the jungle. When she asked Marlow to tell her Kurtz's last words, Marlow hesitated—and then lied, saying, "The last word he pronounced was—your name." The Intended sighed and wept. Marlow's tale is over. On board the *Nellie*, the anonymous narrator and the other men sit motionless. The narrator looks at the dark clouds, the overcast sky, and the Thames—which he now sees as flowing "into the heart of an immense darkness."

Commentary

Theme

Throughout Parts 1 and 2 of *Heart of Darkness*, Kurtz is a shadowy figure whose name is dropped at different times and whose personality and importance eludes both Marlow and the reader. Only after reading Part 3, however, does Kurtz's overall importance become clear and Conrad's design show itself; the novel is about the meeting of two men (Marlow and Kurtz) whose existences mirror each other. Ultimately, Conrad suggests that Kurtz is who Marlow *may* become if he abandons all restraint while working in the jungle. Part 3 emphasizes Kurtz's godlike stature to show *why* Kurtz became what he did and *how* Marlow retreats from this fate.

Throughout Part 3, Conrad stresses the absolute devotion that Kurtz inspires in his followers. The Harlequin, for example, speaks with enthusiasm when speaking of Kurtz: "He made me see things—things," he tells Marlow, and adds, "You can't judge Kurtz as you would an ordinary man." This is an important statement, because it reflects the idea that Kurtz feels he has moved beyond the judgement of his fellow man. By abandoning himself to his innermost desires and lusts, Kurtz has achieved a god-like status. Note that this god-like status is not simply an illusion in Kurtz's mind, for the heads of neighboring tribes fall prostrate before Kurtz and, more surprisingly, the very natives being forced into slavery by the Company attack Marlow's steamboat because they do not want Kurtz to leave. The sight later on of the three natives covered in earth and the "wild woman" reinforce Kurtz's godlike stature.

"He came to them with thunder and lightning," the Harlequin explains, "and they had never seen anything like it." Fulfilling what Conrad saw as the wish of many Europeans, Kurtz has established himself as a violent force, ready to extract vengeance on anyone who disobeys his commands.

Ironically, however, Kurtz does not appear to fit this description physically. Pale, emaciated, and weak, he is often referred to by Marlow as a shadow of a man, a man who is "hollow at the core" and who actually longs for his own destruction. In essence, succumbing to what Marlow calls the "various lusts" that can possess any man has taken its toll on Kurtz's soul—a toll that is reflected in Kurtz's withered frame. Once a formidable tyrant, Kurtz is now "an animated image of death carved out of old ivory." As Kurtz's "wild woman" is a personification of the jungle Kurtz himself is the embodiment of the Company: a force that revels in its own power for power's sake. (Recall how Kurtz turned his canoe around after coming two hundred miles down the river; after tasting the power that his position afforded him, Kurtz could not return to the confining "civilization" of Europe.)

Besides implying the idea that Kurtz embodies the Company, the passage is important because it suggests that even men with "great plans" such as Kurtz (recall his painting and ideas about how each station should be a "beacon on the road to better things") can discover they are, in fact, exactly like the "savages" they are purporting to "save." Underneath the sheen of "civilization," there exists, in every man, a core of brutality. Many people manage to suppress this part of themselves, but Kurtz chose to court it instead. His previous beliefs and "plans" really meant nothing—there was no substance to them, which is why Marlow calls Kurtz "hollow at the core." Kurtz's report on "Savage Customs" reflects this duality—its opening pages are filled with grandiose plans for reform, but its author's true feelings are revealed in his postscript, "Exterminate all the brutes!"

Character Insight

It is Kurtz's abandoning all previously cherished codes of conduct and morality that strikes Marlow as so fascinating. No longer pretending to be a force of "civilization" (as the Company does), Kurtz has moved beyond the confines of modern morality and ideas about right and wrong. When Marlow says that Kurtz "had kicked himself loose of the earth," he is metaphorically implying that Kurtz broke free from the restraints of the basic morality (a sense of right and wrong) that creates order in the world—but Marlow then qualifies this idea with, "Confound the man! he had kicked the very earth to pieces." In other words, Kurtz has not created a new code of conduct or morality—he has dismissed the very *idea* of morality altogether. This is why Marlow cannot "appeal" to him in the name of country, finance, or even humanity. Like Frankenstein's creature, Kurtz is *in* the world but not *of* it.

The Company wants to get rid of Kurtz because he reveals the lie to their methods. He collects more ivory than any other agent because he uses absolute brute force in collecting it and never hides his real intentions behind the kind of philosophy espoused by Marlow's aunt in Part 1. The Company, however, does not want to appear "loose from the earth" like their number-one agent, which is why its representatives (the Manager and the spectacled man who accosts Marlow in Brussels about Kurtz's papers) want to ensure that Europeans never learn the truth about him. Marlow, while not admiring Kurtz's "methods," does appreciate how Kurtz was able to journey into that part of himself that he (and the rest of us) suppress. According to Marlow, Kurtz was a note-worthy man because "he had made that last stride, he had stepped over the edge, while I had been permitted to draw back my hesitating foot." Kurtz is not heroic, but he is more of an adventurer than Marlow ever imagined he could be—instead of voyaging into an unknown conti-nent, he voyaged into the unknown parts of his own soul. For this alone, Marlow feels the need to safeguard Kurtz's reputation, because no one who had not made such a journey into himself could ever possibly understand Kurtz's.

What Kurtz himself thinks of his own actions and "kicking the earth to pieces" is much more difficult to pinpoint; his final words—"The horror! The horror!"—have elicited an enormous amount of critical commentary. Marlow suggests that these words reflect Kurtz's "supreme moment of complete knowledge"—an epiphany in which Kurtz saw exactly what succumbing to his own darkness had done to him. Care should be taken, however, not to read Kurtz's finals words as an apol-ogy or deathbed retraction of his life. *Heart of Darkness* is not a fable, and one of its themes is that the darkness courted by Kurtz is poten-tially in everyone's heart—not just the one belonging to this "voracious" demagogue. Kurtz may be commenting on the force for which he has given his life, or the fact that he will not live long enough to finish his "great plans." Conrad's deliberately ambiguous choice of Kurtz's dying words allows for a number of interpretations while simultaneously refus-ing the reader the comfort he or she would feel in reducing Kurtz to neat categories and descriptions. Like Africa, Kurtz is mysterious, and the workings of his heart at his "supreme moment" remain mysterious as well.

Still, the only character remotely aware of what Kurtz did and what drove him is Marlow, which is why, upon his return to Europe, he finds the people there to be "intruders whose knowledge of life" is "an irritating pretence." He finds them "offensive" because of their self-assuredness in their morals and belief in the inherent "rightness" of their civilization—a "rightness" Marlow now scorns because he sees it (like the Company's wish to bring the "light of civilization" into Africa) as a façade. This is why, in the opening pages of his narrative, Marlow speaks of the Romans conquering England, which "has been one of the dark places of the earth." Marlow now understands that empires are not built without the kinds of activities he witnessed in the Congo and that the "civilization" that is held in such esteem is, in a sense, "just robbery with violence, aggravated murder on a grand scale, and men going at it blind." While Marlow never wishes to abandon civilization in favor of the path chosen by Kurtz, he can no longer view it with the same enthusiasm and comfort that he did before working for the Company. Kurtz has taught him too much.

The final meeting between Marlow and Kurtz's Intended dramatizes this conflict in Marlow's heart. The Intended (who knows little about the real Kurtz) contrasts Kurtz's native mistress (who presumably knew intimately of his "various lusts") and brings to mind the duality of Kurtz's character. Dressed in mourning for over a year, she too, suggests the complete devotion of Kurtz's followers: "For her he had died only yesterday." Her black mourning dress, "ashen halo," and dark eyes bring to mind the numerous examples of light and dark imagery throughout the novel—except that here, the images are more pronounced than anywhere else in the book. The Intended's "darkness" reflects her own sorrow at the loss of her love, but Marlow attempts to hide a greater and more threatening darkness: The truth about Kurtz.

Marlow is not deliberately trying to be sarcastic by repeating the Intended's words; the irony of the naïve Intended presuming to "know Kurtz best" is what gives Marlow's repetitions their bite.

As Marlow struggles to maintain his composure, he notices the physical and metaphorical darkness that permeates the room. He arrives at the Intended's house at dusk. At the beginning of the conversation, he notices the room "growing darker" and only her forehead remaining "illuminated by the inextinguishable light of belief and love." When she begins explaining that she knew Kurtz better than anyone else, Marlow comments, "The darkness deepened" and, in his heart, bows his head before her. The truth about Kurtz—metaphorically represented in the coming of night—becomes more difficult for Marlow to hide, because the Intended's presumed knowledge of Kurtz becomes more unnerving to him as they continue. After the "last gleams of twilight" fall, Marlow even admits to feeling some "dull anger" at her naiveté, but this feeling turns to "infinite pity" when Marlow realizes the immensity of her ignorance. This is why, when asked to repeat Kurtz's final words, Marlow cannot bring himself to repeat, "The horror! The horror!" and instead tells a lie that gives great comfort to the Intended while simultaneously securing Kurtz's reputation. Despite the fact that Marlow knows that lies are wrong, he cannot refrain from telling this one, because to do so "would have been too dark—too dark altogether." As the Intended gratefully receives Marlow's lie, so Europe accepts the one it tells itself about building empires and civilizing "savages."

Glossary

ulster a long, loose, heavy overcoat, especially one with a belt, originally made of Irish frieze (wool).

the first of the ebb the start of the outgoing or falling tide.

CHARACTER ANALYSES

Marlow

Marlow is a thirty-two-year-old sailor that has always lived at sea. The novel's narrator presents Marlow as "a meditating Buddha" because his experiences in the Congo have made him introspective and to a certain degree philosophic and wise. As a young man, Marlow wished to explore the "blank places" on the map because he longed for adventure; his journey up the Congo, however, proves to be much more than a thrilling episode. Instead, his experiences there teach Marlow about the "heart of darkness" found in all men: Many (like himself) suppress these evil urges, while others (like Kurtz) succumb to them.

Marlow's chief qualities are his curiosity and skepticism. Never easily satisfied with others' seemingly innocent remarks such as those made by the Manager and Brickmaker, Marlow constantly attempts to sift through the obscurities of what others tell him (such as when his aunt speaks to him of "weaning those ignorant millions from their horrid ways"). However, Marlow is no crusader for Truth. He lies to Kurtz's Intended to save her from a broken heart and ultimately returns to Europe and his home, despite his having been convinced by the Company and Kurtz that civilization is, ultimately, a lie and an institution humans have created to channel their desires for power.

As *Heart of Darkness* progresses, Marlow becomes increasingly sensitive to his surroundings and the "darkness" that they may embody or hide. When he visits the Company's headquarters, for example, he is slightly alarmed by the doctor's comments and puzzled by the two women knitting black wool. When he arrives at the Outer Station, however, he is shocked at the amount of waste and disregard for life he sees there. By the end of the novel, Marlow is almost unable to reintegrate himself into European society, having become convinced of the lies and "surface-truths" that sustain it. He tells his story to the men aboard the *Nellie* to share with them what he has learned about the darkness of the human heart—and the things of which that darkness is capable.

Kurtz

One of the most enigmatic characters in twentieth-century literature, Kurtz is a petty tyrant, a dying god, an embodiment of Europe, and an assault on European values. These contradictory elements combine to make Kurtz so fascinating to Marlow—and so threatening to the Company.

Like Marlow, Kurtz also wished to travel to Africa in search of adventure—specifically, to complete great acts of "humanizing, improving, instructing" (as he explains in his initial report to the Company). Once he tasted the power that could be his in the jungle, however, Kurtz abandoned his philanthropic ideals and set himself up as a god to the natives at the Inner Station. While he used to worry about the best ways to bring (as his painting demonstrates) the "light" of civilization to the Congo, he dies as a man believing that the Company should simply "Exterminate all the brutes!"

Kurtz is a dangerous man because he gives the lie to the Company's "humanistic" intentions in the Congo. He returns more ivory than all the other stations put together, and does so through the use of absolute force. This frightens men like the Manager, who complains of Kurtz's "unsound method"—although Kurtz is only doing what the Company as a whole is doing *without* hiding his actions behind a façade of good intentions. Marlow remarks that "All Europe contributed to the making of Kurtz," and Kurtz's very existence proves this to be true: Like the Europeans involved in enterprises such as the Company, he epitomizes the greed and lust running wild that Marlow observes in the Congo. However, unlike the Company, Kurtz is not interested in his image or how he is perceived by "noxious fools" such as the Manager. While Brussels is a "whited sepulcher" of hypocrisy, Kurtz is completely open about his lusts. He tells the Manager he is "Not so sick as you'd like to believe." But this statement is applicable to all Europeans involved in imperialistic empire-building: While labeling Kurtz a morally "sick" man might seem comforting, he is actually an exaggeration of the impulses harbored in the hearts of men everywhere.

The Manager

As Kurtz (in some sense) embodies Europe, the Manager embodies the Company that he represents in the Congo. The Manager's primary concern is preserving his position within the Company, which he incorrectly assumes Kurtz wishes to steal from him. A scheming liar, the Manager sabotages Marlow's steamboat to prevent supplies from reaching Kurtz at the Inner Station. Neither Marlow nor Kurtz believe his shows of concern for Kurtz's health: When he tells Kurtz that he has come to save him, Kurtz replies, "Save the ivory, you mean," and after Kurtz dies, Marlow feels the Manager's eyes on him as he leaves Kurtz's room, eager to learn of his rival agent's death. According to Marlow, the

Manager "inspires uneasiness" and tries to use this ability to gain information about Kurtz and his activities from Marlow. A despicable man, the Manager has the power to make the Company a reputable operation, but refuses to do so for fear that this would impede the flow of ivory that comes out of Africa.

The Accountant

Although he only appears in the novel for a short time, the Accountant is an important figure because he personifies the Company's goals and methods. The fact that he spends his days with his ledger in the middle of the jungle suggests the great importance the Company places on profits. Moreover, his immaculately white and spotless dress suggests the Company's desire to seem "morally spotless" to the rest of the world. When a dying man is brought into his hut, the Accountant complains, "The groans of this sick person distract my attention. And without that it is extremely difficult to guard against clerical errors in this climate." Like the Company, the Accountant wants men to die out of eyesight so he can focus his "attention" on preventing "clerical errors." Sickness and death are inevitable parts of business, and if one dwells on them they are liable to "distract" him from his main purpose: Tallying the profits. Ironically, these profits are supposed to be used to help the natives that the Company is destroying.

The Accountant also hints at the great hatred that the Whites have for the natives, as well as the fact that there are agents at the Central Station who will do anything to further their own careers.

The Harlequin

This Russian disciple of Kurtz is so named by Marlow because of the different-colored patches he wears on his clothes. The image of a clown in motley dress also suggests the Harlequin's position as Kurtz's "court jester." Despite the fact that Kurtz threatened to kill him, the Harlequin can only offer effusive praise of Kurtz's intellect, charisma, and wisdom. When Marlow first meets him, the Harlequin serves as a possible outcome of Marlow's journey: Will he remain his skeptical self or fall prey to the same "magic" that enraptured this man? The Harlequin says of Kurtz, "This man has enlarged my mind"; like Marlow, he finds Kurtz's voice fascinating, shocking, and compelling.

The Intended

Kurtz's fiancée is marked—like the Harlequin—by her absolute devotion to Kurtz. When Marlow visits her after his return from Africa, he finds that she has been dressed in mourning for more than a year and still yearns for information about how her love spent his last days. However, she is actually devoted to an *image* of Kurtz instead of the man himself: She praises Kurtz's "words" and "example," assuming that these are filled with the nobility of purpose with which Kurtz began his career with the Company. Her devotion is so absolute that Marlow cannot bear to tell her Kurtz's real last words ("The horror! The horror!") and must instead tell her a lie that strengthens her already false impression of Kurtz. On a symbolic level, the Intended is like many Europeans, who wish to believe in the greatness of men like Kurtz without considering the more "dark" and hidden parts of their characters. Like European missionaries, for example, who sometimes hurt the very people they were professing to save, the Intended is a misguided soul whose belief in Marlow's lie reveals her need to cling to a fantasy-version of the what the Europeans (i.e., the Company) are doing in Africa.

Kurtz's Native Mistress

The Congolese woman that rails against Kurtz's departure is a complete contrast to Kurtz's Intended. As the Intended is innocent and naïve, the native mistress is bold and powerful. Kurtz is a man of many lusts, and she embodies this part of his personality. She frightens the Harlequin because she finds him to be meddling with Kurtz too much; her threats to him eventually scare him into leaving the Inner Station.

Fresleven

Although he is only mentioned in one section of the novel, Fresleven reflects the power of the jungle on seemingly civilized men. Before he left for Africa, Fresleven was described as a kind and gentle man; after being exposed to the Congo, however, he became savage and was killed in a meaningless quarrel with a native chief. The grass that Marlow saw growing through his bones suggests the power of the jungle over civilized men. Like the Harlequin, Fresleven is presented as one possible outcome for Marlow on his journey up the Congo River.

CRITICAL ESSAYS

Conrad's Use of the Frame Tale

First-time readers of *Heart of Darkness* may be initially puzzled by Conrad's decision to have Marlow's story told to the reader by the anonymous narrator who listens to Marlow on the deck of the *Nellie*. Such a reader may wonder why Conrad would make *Heart of Darkness* a **frame tale** at all and not simply begin with Marlow telling the story, as many first-person narratives do. The reason is that Conrad's frame narrator, like the reader, learns that his ideas about European imperialism are founded on a number of lies that he has wholeheartedly believed. By the end of the novel, Marlow's tale significantly changes the narrator's attitude toward the ships and men of the past.

Heart of Darkness begins not on a steamboat fighting its way upriver in the Congo, but on the deck of a "cruising yawl"—a boat used more for domestic trade than overseas imperial conquests. All is still: The sails do not flutter, the tide has subsided and the wind is "nearly calm." Immediately the reader sees a contrast between the serene European setting and the chaotic and threatening African landscape described later.

The narrator begins speaking as the day is drawing to a close; his descriptions of the sky and weather suggest both beauty and mystery. While his descriptions contribute to the atmosphere aboard the *Nellie*, they also reflect the moral "haze" and "mist" in which Marlow finds himself as he journeys closer and closer to Kurtz. The afternoon is thus like the tale that Marlow will tell: ambiguous, brooding, and, above all, "dark."

Note that the narrator remarks that for Marlow, "the meaning of an episode was not inside like a kernel but outside, enveloping the talk which brought it out only as a glow brings out a haze." This is an important description of Marlow's—and, by extension, Conrad's—technique: *Heart of Darkness* is as much "about" a man's witnessing horror as much as it concerns the same man's struggle to put his experiences into words. The *way* that Marlow tells his tale, therefore, is as much a part of the novel as the tale itself. Sentences such as this description of the jungle— "It was the stillness of an implacable force brooding over an inscrutable intention"—and this one about Kurtz's Report to the Society for the Suppression of Savage Customs—"It gave me the notion of an exotic Immensity ruled by an august Benevolence"—thus demonstrate Marlow's inability to fully articulate the *exact* meaning of what he saw in the Congo. Like the sky above the *Nellie*, Marlow's language sometimes becomes "hazy" and fails to illuminate the very subjects that his language is presumably trying to clarify.

Before Marlow speaks, however, Conrad allows the reader to glimpse the narrator's values and assumptions. He first speaks of the Thames as a "venerable stream" that exists to perform "unceasing service" to those who have tamed it: "The old river in its broad reach rested unruffled at the decline of day, after ages of good service done to the race that peopled its banks." To the narrator, nature exists to serve mankind, especially mankind's commerce and trade. This idea of mankind's dominance over the earth is questioned by Marlow later in the novel, as he looks out at the jungle and asks, "What were we that had strayed in here? Could we handle that dumb thing, or would it handle us? I felt how big, how confoundedly big, was that thing that couldn't talk, and perhaps was deaf as well. What was in there?" Conrad's reason for framing Marlow's narrative thus begins to become apparent: The narrator's values and assumptions are challenged—although indirectly—by Marlow's story, and the reader is meant to perceive these two points-of-view as two different understandings of man's relationship to the natural world and the people in it. Although the narrator states that the Thames leads "to the uttermost ends of the earth," he never imagines that his civilized London could ever have been (as Marlow calls it), "one of the dark places of the earth."

Such a contrast between the narrator and Marlow's attitudes is more readily seen in the way the narrator speaks of what he sees as England's glorious past. According to him, the Thames is a river that has served the nation in efforts of both trade and exploration. The narrator finds glory and pride in his nation's past, assured in his knowledge that "knight-errants" of the sea have brought "sparks from the sacred fire" of civilization to the most remote corners of the earth. While these "knights" may have resorted to the "sword," they have also passed the "torch," and, in doing so, made the world a more prosperous and civilized place. (Recall the painting by Kurtz that Marlow sees at the Central Station.) The narrator knows the men and their ships and speaks of them in a reverential tone. Europe's past is the history of brave adventurers conquering the unknown, and, in the process, transforming "the dreams of men" into "the seeds of commonwealths" and "the germs of empires."

Clearly, this vision of Europe as a civilizing and "torch-bearing" force does not accord with Marlow's portrayal of it in his narrative. While institutions like the Company may *ostensibly* wish to help the less fortunate peoples of the earth (as Kurtz's Report to the Society for the Suppression of Savage Customs and his painting in the Accountant's office suggest), Marlow learns that the narrator's version of imperialism is a lie. The Europeans he meets are not "knight-errants" but "faithless pilgrims"; the Company does not bring a "spark from that sacred fire," but death, and instead of a bright "jewel," flashing "in the night of time," the Company is a "rapacious" and "weak-eyed devil." Marlow's story thus challenges the reader—who may hold some of the same opinions as the narrator—to view the men of the Company not as men engaged in a great mission, but instead as men engaged in "a weary pilgrimage amongst hints for nightmares."

At the end of the novel Marlow's tale has significantly changed the narrator's attitude toward European imperialism. The narrator compares him to "a meditating Buddha"—clearly he has been touched by Marlow's teachings. While the Director of Companies remarks, "We have lost the flow of the ebb" because he wants to break the uncomfortable silence created by the power of Marlow's story, the narrator has been too affected by Marlow's ideas, and his enlightenment affects his description of what he sees as he looks at the Thames: a dark river leading to "an immense darkness."

The Director of Companies remains aloof, since his living is made presumably by the same horrific processes that Marlow has just described. Only the narrator—and the reader—understand Marlow's initial point: "Civilized" Europe was once also a "dark place," and it has only become more morally dark through the activities of institutions such as the Company.

Apocalypse Now

Apocalypse Now is director Francis Ford Coppola's film based on *Heart of Darkness* but set in the jungles of Vietnam. While some critics found the film belabored and muddled, most agreed that it was a powerful and important examination not only of America's military involvement in Vietnam, but like Conrad's novel, a disturbing treatment of the darkness potentially inherent in all human hearts. "Apocalypse" means the end of the world, as when the earth is destroyed by fire in the Bible. As the film's title suggests, Coppola explores the ways in which the metaphorical "darkness" of Vietnam causes an apocalypse in the hearts of those sent there to fight.

Coppola retained the basic structure of Conrad's novel for his film. As *Heart of Darkness* follows Marlow's journey through the different Company stations and eventually upriver to Kurtz, Coppola's film moves in an analogous way. The protagonist is an Army Captain (Willard) who receives his orders, gathers his crew, and creeps up the Nung River until he meets and assassinates a renegade soldier (Col. Walter Kurtz). Both the Company and the Army want their "Kurtzes" dead, because both Kurtzes detest and expose their superiors' motives and methods. Their willingness to go all the way terrifies their superiors, who do not want to be so blatantly reminded of their *real* goals (ivory in the *Heart of Darkness* and power in *Apocalypse Now*) and methods of attaining them.

Like Conrad's Company, Coppola's Army is a disorganized band of men whose hypocrisy is questioned by the central characters. As the Company masquerades as a philanthropic and humane institution bringing "light" to Africa (recall Kurtz's painting), the Army (as embodied by General Corman and Colonel Lucas, the men who give Willard his mission) pretends to be greatly disturbed by the fact that Col. Kurtz has broken from their command and begun fighting the war in his own way. The Army has charged Col. Kurtz with the murder of four Vietnamese double agents, which is the ostensible reason why they want to "terminate" his command. Willard, however, sees through their façade and remarks to himself, "Charging someone for murder out here was like handing out speeding tickets at the Indy 500." As the Manager feigns great concern over Kurtz's health in *The Heart of Darkness*, General Corman acts pained and upset when he tells Willard, "Every man has a breaking point. Walter Kurtz has obviously reached his."

More striking than the parallels in plot, however, are those of character. As Marlow's jaunt to Africa becomes much more to him than an adventure, so does Willard's mission to kill Col. Kurtz become more than an order: "When it was done," he explains, "I'd never want another." Both become wiser yet more shaken as a result of their journeys, and both tell their stories (Marlow on the *Nellie*, Willard in his voice-overs) to teach their listeners about their discoveries concerning the "hearts of darkness" into which they traveled.

Willard, like Marlow, becomes more perceptive to the moral darkness around him as the film proceeds. An important difference between these characters, however, is that Willard *begins* the film as a man already accustomed to the "horror" around him. The opening shots of the film reveal Willard in a Saigon hotel; on his nightstand is a gun (he has already considered suicide) and he explains, in a voice-over, that he was unable to adjust to life in the United States after his first tour of duty. Coppola then presents the viewer with a montage of Willard screaming, crying, and smashing a mirror to show how desperately Willard needs a mission to give his life some purpose. Another difference is that Marlow wanted to explore "the blank places" on a map to satisfy his thirst for adventure, but Willard needs a mission so that he doesn't become (as he fears) "weaker."

The problem Col. Kurtz poses to the Army deserves further investigation. Like Conrad's Kurtz, he was a "prodigy": a Green Beret, paratrooper, and candidate for a position with the Joint Chiefs of Staff. Willard also learns that Kurtz organized a covert operation ("Archangel") without the permission of his superiors—an operation which might have brought him court-martial, but instead earned him a promotion to Colonel once the news of it was made public. As the war continued, Kurtz kept winning battles and becoming stronger—and it was this strength that made him threatening to the Army, just as Conrad's Kurtz (who brings in more ivory than all other stations combined) unnerves the Manager. Just as "All Europe contributed to the making of Kurtz" in that he embodied many of the Europeans' values about the white man's power over the natives, so has "all America" contributed to the making of Col. Kurtz—a man who once personified the traditional American values of strength and valor, but who became—once he glimpsed the darkness of war—someone who could not uphold the hypocrisy of which he was once a major part.

Willard reads a letter from Col. Kurtz to his son that reveals his hatred of the system that once extolled him. Col. Kurtz explains that while the Army has accused him of murdering the four Vietnamese double-agents, the charges are, "in the circumstances of this conflict, quite completely insane." He continues:

"In a war, there are many moments for compassion and tender action. There are many moments for ruthless action. What is often called "ruthless" . . . may, in many circumstances, be only clarity: Seeing clearly what there is to be done and dong it—directly, quickly, looking at it."

Col. Kurtz feels that in murdering the double agents, he was simply exhibiting a soldier's "clarity": The agents were captured, they were enemies, and were therefore killed. What Kurtz detests is the Army's purposeful *lack* of "clarity": He knows that they cannot (in this war) afford to appear "ruthless" and are therefore attempting to smear his name and color his actions as insane. Col. Kurtz ends his letter with an expression of his hatred of lies: "As for the charges against me, I am unconcerned; I am above their timid, lying morality and so I am beyond caring." Later, Col. Kurtz remarks, "We train young men to drop fire on people but will not allow them to write 'fuck' on their airplanes, because it's 'obscene.'" This hypocrisy enrages Kurtz to the point where he can no longer abide by the "timid" moral guidelines of the Army, just as Conrad's Kurtz can no longer abide by the "methods" suggested to him by the Company. Both men detest the lies of their superiors: Recall Kurtz's remark to the Manager when he arrives at the Inner Station to "rescue" him: "Save me!—save the ivory, you mean. Don't tell me. Save *me*!" His subsequent remark to the Manager about his health ("Not so sick as you'd like to believe") is the equivalent of Col. Kurtz's letter: Both the Company and Army want to pretend that their "Kurtzes" are insane rather than admit the truth, which is that both men see their respective organizations for what they truly are.

When Willard meets Kurtz in the last part of the film, Coppola stresses Kurtz's power—but also the weariness that this power has created in Kurtz. Willard is taken prisoner and kept in a cage; on a rainy night, Willard is awakened by Kurtz, who drops the head of one of Willard's crew in his lap, as if to say, "This is what I am capable of doing on a whim." After this show of force, however, Kurtz begins nursing Willard back to health, and Coppola eventually makes clear the idea that Kurtz knows Willard's mission and—more importantly—wants him to carry it out. "If I was still alive it was only because *he* wanted it that way," Willard remarks. Like Kurtz in *Heart of Darkness*, Col. Kurtz cannot sustain his life of exhausting emptiness. Both Kurtzes succumb to the temptation of "forgotten and brutal instincts"—and both find that their lives become "hollow" as a result. As he approaches Col. Kurtz with a machete, Willard's voice-over explains, "Everyone wanted me to do it," including the jungle, "Which is who he really took his orders from." Col. Kurtz wants to die, because after learning what he did about himself, he needs (as Willard explains), "Someone to take the pain away." When Willard kills him, Col. Kurtz offers little resistance; Coppola intersperses the scene of Col. Kurtz's murder with the sacrifice of a bull to suggest that Col. Kurtz is "sacrificed" for the sins of the Army. Eventually, he speaks the same final words as his counterpart with the same ambiguous effect.

After Willard kills Col. Kurtz, he leaves the hut, machete in hand, and sees hundreds of Kurtz's followers bow to him as he walks to his boat. Before he begins his return, however, Willard hesitates, for he has the chance to become Kurtz's successor. After a moment, however, he returns to the boat and the small amount of safety it provides. Thus, in both *Heart of Darkness* and *Apocalypse Now*, both protagonists learn the same lesson: Even a man as "enlightened" and revered as Kurtz can succumb to his dark side if he is freed from the restraints of society. Both protagonists are also able to retreat from the fate that awaited Kurtz— but both of them also come face-to-face with "an impenetrable darkness" that challenges their most basic moral beliefs. Without having met their respective Kurtzes, both men would have found the world less dark than they do at the time of their narrations. But as both Conrad and Coppola suggest, one cannot "unsee" what he has already glimpsed— Marlow and Willard can pull back their feet, but will never forget what lay over the edge.

CLIFFSNOTES REVIEW

Use this CliffsNotes Review to test your understanding of the original text, and reinforce what you've learned in this book. After you work through the review and essay questions, identify the quote section, and the fun and useful practice projects, you're well on your way to understanding a comprehensive and meaningful interpretation of *Heart of Darkness*.

Q & A

1. Marlow originally yearns to visit the Congo in order to

   a. explore the wilderness

   b. amass a great fortune

   c. enlighten the natives

   d. all of the above

2. While cruising up the Congo, Marlow admires the cannibal crewmen's

   a. strength

   b. intelligence

   c. restraint

   d. eloquence

3. Marlow's relief mission to Kurtz is partially sabotaged by

   a. the Accountant

   b. the Manager

   c. the Intended

   d. the Helmsman

Answers: (1) a. (2) c. (3) b.

Identify the Quote

1. "What greatness had not floated on the ebb of that river into the mystery of an unknown earth! . . . The dreams of men, the seed of commonwealths, the germs of empires."

2. "When one has got to make correct entries, one comes to hate those savages—hate them to the death."

3. "We were wanderers on a prehistoric earth, on an earth that wore the aspect of an unknown planet."

4. "This man has enlarged my mind."

5. "The horror! The horror!"

6. "The last word he pronounced was—your name."

Answers: (1) [The narrator at the beginning of the novel; this statement reflects his initial endorsement of European imperialism.] (2) [The Accountant at the Outer Station, who reflects the great importance the Company places on profits.] (3) [Marlow as treks further through the Congo; the quote reflects his removal from civilization.] (4) [The Harlequin when talking to Marlow about Kurtz; here, he reveals his total devotion to Kurtz.] (5) [Kurtz's dying words on Marlow's steamboat; these words are thought by Marlow as an act of self-judgment.] (6) [Marlow, lying to Kurtz's Intended about Kurtz's last words; he tells her this to shield her from the awful truth of what Kurtz became in the jungle.]

Essay Questions

1. How is Marlow's journey up the Congo River a metaphorical journey into himself? Explore the ways he grows and changes during his journey.

2. Compare and contrast Marlow and Kurtz: What does each man initially assume about the Company and Africa? How do these assumptions change?

3. Discuss Conrad's use of light and dark (including black and white) imagery in the novel.

4. Explain why Conrad would write the novel as a frame tale.

5. Compare and contrast Marlow and Willard (the protagonist of *Apocalypse Now*). How does each man face the "heart of darkness" that he encounters in Kurtz?

Practice Projects

1. Research the history of the Belgian Congo and King Leopold II's role in its colonization. Then create a portfolio of different writings from reporters, explorers, and other eyewitnesses that reveal the accuracy of Conrad's depictions of the horrors faced by the Congolese.

2. Design a web site that allows its user to undergo a "virtual journey" up the Congo River that mirrors the one Marlow undertakes in the novel. Along the way, the user should be offered quotations from the novel, as well as links to historical and literary sites.

3. Much has been written about Francis Ford Coppola's *Apocalypse Now*. Research some of the difficulties he faced in bringing Conrad's novel to the screen, and prepare a presentation explaining how these difficulties were met.

INTRODUCTION TO THE STORY

Introduction

"The Secret Sharer" was published in 1910, eight years after the publication of Conrad's *Heart of Darkness*. Like *Heart of Darkness*, the story is based on an actual incident, with some of the facts altered to suit Conrad's artistic purposes: In the 1880s, a mate aboard the *Cutty Sark* killed an insubordinate sailor during an altercation in which the insubordinate sailor eventually died. Like Leggatt, the killer who escapes punishment and befriends the story's narrator, the murderer escaped his punishment by swimming to a new destiny. As he does in *Heart of Darkness*, Conrad uses the story of a sailor to explore themes of great scope.

The story can also be read as a *bildungsroman*—a tale of a young man's coming of age, much like Mark Twain's *The Adventures of Huckleberry Finn*, Charles Dickens's *David Copperfield*, or James Joyce's *A Portrait of the Artist as a Young Man*. Examining the story in light of these deeper levels of meaning transforms the work from a typical adventure story to an allegorical work, rich in symbolism. (The allegorical aspects of the story are examined in detail in Critical Essay 1.)

The Doppelganger Theme

Upon an initial reading, "The Secret Sharer" seems to be an old-fashioned tale of adventure on the sea. The story features a captain, his crew, a mysterious event, a murder, a near-disaster, and the saving of a ship. While "The Secret Sharer" is an adventure yarn, it also stands as a profound and often disquieting examination of every person's dual nature and how each person must resolve this duality for the self to grow. Conrad's use of the *doppelganger theme*—a character's double or alter-ego—allows him to explore the dual nature of his protagonist, a young yet unsure captain assuming his first command. (The *doppelganger theme* is also found in *Heart of Darkness*, where Kurtz represents, on a symbolic level, the darkness in Marlow that he struggles to suppress.)

"The Secret Sharer" concerns a young captain who assumes the command of his ship only a fortnight before the action of the story begins. Because of this, he is doubtful, untried, and feels himself at the mercy of a crew that while not mutinous or even hostile, slightly undermines the authority that a captain should possess if he is to truly command a ship as he sees fit. Like the skipper of the *Sephora* (the ship from which

Leggatt escaped), the Captain worries over his reputation and the means by which he can preserve it during his first command. Because he lacks the courage and conviction needed to command a ship successfully, he stands as a well-meaning yet weak example of a typical captain. Once Leggatt appears from the depths of the sea—a possible symbol of the Captain's unconscious desire to remedy his own weaknesses—the Captain's personality begins to change.

His discovery of Leggatt changes the Captain in both obvious and subtle ways. Leggatt is, by definition, a killer who murdered an insolent sailor while simultaneously saving the *Sephora* during a terrible storm. While Leggatt did not intentionally kill the seaman, he is still a powerful and slightly sinister figure. Thus, Leggatt (a renegade from the law) represents the more brutal, irrational side of man, while the Captain represents the more civilized and refined one. Although the Captain thinks that a ship should be run in an orderly and straightforward fashion, Leggatt struck the insolent seaman because he would not assist him in repairing a sail. This is hardly an orderly action to take, but Leggatt felt no regard for rules and regulations when the lives of his fellow sailors were at stake during the storm, and the insolent seaman refused to cooperate in repairing the sail. The Captain, therefore, represents the more rational but timid side of humankind, while Leggatt represents the more irrational but brave side. Together, the Captain and Leggatt make up a perfect commander, and Conrad's story tracks how Leggatt influences the Captain and by doing so, transforms him into the perfect commander.

Conrad's use of the *doppelganger theme* invites the reader to consider his or her own duality, and to struggle for a balance between the rational and irrational, the timid and bold, the public and private sides of his or her personality. According to "The Secret Sharer," one's personality is created through interacting with others who offer a glimpse into the part of oneself that one assumes he or she lacks, only to discover that it has been lying dormant, waiting to be released.

A Brief Synopsis

"The Secret Sharer" begins with the anonymous narrator—the recently appointed captain of an unnamed ship—anchored in the Gulf of Siam (what is now called the Gulf of Thailand). As the Captain stands on the deck, alone, he soaks in the sunset and silence of the sea. He feels like a stranger to his new command, the ship, and his crew.

At supper that night, the Captain remarks that he saw the masts of a ship that must be anchored inside a nearby group of islands. The Second Mate tells him that the ship is the *Sephora*, from Liverpool, carrying a cargo of coal. As a goodwill gesture toward the crew, who have been working hard the last two days, the Captain announces that he will take the anchor watch until 1:00 a.m., something usually not done by a ship's captain.

During the anchor watch, while the hands are asleep, the Captain begins to pull in the rope side ladder, which was lowered for a tugboat man to come on board and deliver the crew's mail. When he begins to pull it in, he feels a jerk in the ropes, and surprised, leans over the deck to investigate. He sees a naked man in the water, holding the bottom of the ladder. The man introduces himself as Leggatt, and the Captain fetches him some clothes (one of his sleeping suits). Leggatt explains that he was the *Sephora's* chief mate and that he accidentally killed an insolent fellow crewman seven weeks ago. The Captain takes him into his stateroom and further learns that Leggatt was kept under arrest in his cabin until he escaped and swam to the rope ladder where the Captain discovered him. He sank his clothes so the *Sephora's* crew would think he had committed suicide by drowning.

The Captain feels an unexplainable affinity to Leggatt, often referring to him as "my double" or "second self." The Captain tells Leggatt that he has only been in charge for two weeks and feels as much of a stranger on the ship as Leggatt himself. He agrees to hide Leggatt in his stateroom.

The *Sephora's* captain soon arrives in his search for the escaped murderer. He searches the ship, but Leggatt remains hidden, thanks to the maneuverings of the Captain. The *Sephora's* captain states that he will have to report Leggatt as a suicide when his ship arrives home. The Captain and Leggatt share their relief at not having been caught.

As the Captain's ship begins its voyage home, the Captain grows more nervous about the possibility of the crew discovering Leggatt on board. On the fourth day out, the steward almost stumbles upon Leggatt when he delivers the Captain's coat to his stateroom. Leggatt tells the Captain that he must maroon him amongst some islands, because he knows he cannot return to England and face prison or the gallows. The Captain reluctantly agrees.

As the ship approaches Koh-ring, an island, the Captain orders the crew to steer the ship close to the shore. They protest that such a move is unsafe, but the Captain is determined to give Leggatt a chance to swim to safety. After stealing away to his stateroom and shaking Leggatt's hand, the Captain continues to have the ship steered close to the shore, despite all the protests of his terrified crew. Leggatt jumps off the deck and swims to safety, the Captain successfully maneuvers the ship out of danger, and wishes Leggatt luck in finding his "new destiny."

List of Characters

The Captain The unnamed Captain of an unnamed ship who narrates the story. A young man struggling to prove himself worthy of the command he was given a fortnight before the story begins, he finds Leggatt in the water, hides him in his cabin, and eventually helps him escape to freedom.

Leggatt The "secret sharer" of the Captain's cabin, Leggatt was the chief mate of the *Sephora* until he accidentally killed an insolent crewman during a particularly tense emergency during a storm. Stripped of his command and confined to his room until he could be brought to trial in London, Leggatt broke free from the *Sephora's* confines and swam to the Captain's ship, where he is discovered at the beginning of the story.

The Skipper of the Sephora A weak man bullied by both his crew and his wife, the Skipper of the *Sephora* visits the Captain's ship during his search for Leggatt. He is easily tricked by the Captain into believing that Leggatt drowned during his escape.

The Chief Mate A whiskered man whose "dominant trait was to take all things into earnest consideration," such as the scorpion he found in his inkwell a week before the beginning of the story.

The Second Mate Described by the Captain as a "silent young man, grave beyond his years," the second mate sneers at the Captain's questions about the *Sephora* early in the story. He embodies the undermining of the Captain's command that plagues the Captain until he meets Leggatt.

The Steward The cook on board the Captain's ship. At one point, he almost discovers Leggatt hidden in the Captain's cabin.

Character Map

The Secret Sharer

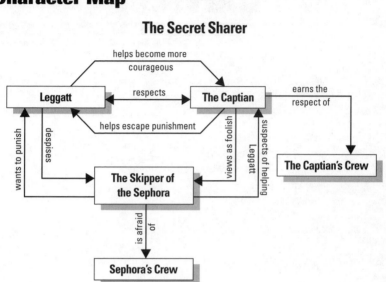

CRITICAL
COMMENTARIES

Part 1

Summary

As dusk begins to fall, the unnamed narrator of the story stands on the deck of his ship, currently anchored at the mouth of the Meinam River in the Gulf of Siam. The narrator is the Captain of the ship who leaves the deck to eat supper with his mates. The time is approximately eight o'clock.

At supper, the Captain remarks that he saw the masts of a ship anchored amongst some nearby islands. The Chief Mate explains that the ship to which the Captain is referring is probably another English one, waiting for the right moment to sail home with a favorable tide. The Second Mate elaborates: The ship is the *Sephora*, from Liverpool, and is bound home from Cardiff with a cargo of coal. (He learned this from the skipper of the tugboat who came aboard to fetch the Captain's letters.)

The Captain makes a magnanimous gesture by offering to take the anchor watch himself until one o'clock, after which time he will get the Second Mate to relieve him. Again alone on deck, the Captain meditatively smokes a cigar and again considers his own "strangeness" to the ship and its command. The rest of the crew sleeps soundly.

The Captain notices that the rope side ladder, hung over the side of the ship to accommodate the skipper of the tugboat, has not been brought in. As he begins to pull it, he feels a jerk at the other end and curious, looks over the rail into the sea. He sees a naked man floating in the water and holding the end of the ladder. The man introduces himself as Leggatt. He has been in the water since nine o'clock, which makes the Captain consider his strength and youth. Leggatt climbs up the ladder and the Captain rushes to his cabin to fetch him some clothes. The Captain learns that Leggatt was the chief mate of the *Sephora* and that he accidentally killed a fellow crewman. Although Leggatt unintentionally murdered the man, the Skipper stripped Leggatt of his title. The Captain tells Leggatt that they should retire to his cabin so as not to be discovered by the Chief Mate. The Captain hides Leggatt in his cabin, returns to the deck, summons the Chief Mate to take over the anchor watch, and returns to his cabin.

Leggatt continues his story: After killing the man, he was placed under arrest and kept in his cabin for almost seven weeks. Approximately six weeks into his confinement, Leggatt asked to see the Skipper and asked him to leave his door unlocked that night, while the *Sephora* sailed through the Sunda Straits, so that he could jump off and swim to the Java coast. The Skipper refused.

Three weeks later, the *Sephora* came to its present location, and Leggatt discovered that the ship's steward—wholly by accident—had left the door to his cabin unlocked. Leggatt wandered onto the deck and jumped off into the sea. He swam to a nearby islet while the *Sephora's* crew lowered a boat to search for him. Leggatt removed his clothes and sank them, determined never to return. He swam to another small island, saw the riding light of the Captain's ship, and swam to it. Eventually, he reached the rope ladder, completely exhausted after swimming over a mile. The Captain helps Leggatt into his bed, where he falls asleep immediately. The Captain eventually falls asleep himself; the next morning, the steward enters the Captain's cabin to bring him his morning coffee. (He does not notice Leggatt because the Captain drew the curtains that separate the bed from the rest of the cabin.) The Captain becomes more paranoid that someone will discover Leggatt and decides that he must show himself on deck. The Captain learns that a ship's boat is coming toward their ship. He orders the ladder to be dropped over the side and leaves Leggatt to meet who he is sure will be the Skipper of the *Sephora*, searching for Leggatt.

Commentary

When the story begins, Conrad implies that the Captain gained his post through connections rather than by steadily rising through the ranks of his fellow sailors. By the end of the story, however, Leggatt helps the Captain become more assured with his command and more respected by his crew.

The Chief Mate's anecdote about finding a scorpion in his inkwell holds symbolic importance. Like the scorpion, found in the most unlikely of places, Leggatt similarly is found clinging to the rope ladder. Leggatt's crime of murder (although accidental) similarly marks him as dangerous, like a scorpion. Finally, Conrad begins employing *color symbolism* here: The scorpion drowns in an inkwell, rendering it black when discovered by the Chief Mate, while Leggatt's hair is black, thus strengthening the connection between these two outcasts: Black is the color most associated with evil in Western thinking, and one should note that both the scorpion and Leggatt are stained black. The scorpion literally by the ink and Leggatt figuratively by his crime.

The Captain's desire to take the anchor watch himself stems from his feelings of isolation and alienation. Although he feels "painfully" that he is "doing something unusual" in taking on the watch himself, he does so to learn more about the ship and what he calls "the novel responsibility of command." He enjoys watching the sea because of its "singleness of purpose." The sea, unlike his own command, makes sense to him in its "absolute straightforwardness."

Leggatt's entrance into the story marks him as an almost supernatural force, sent by some higher power to assist the Captain in his struggle to gain the respect of his men and himself. His naked form and his rising from the sea heighten the suggestion that Leggatt has been "created" for the Captain. Again note Conrad's use of symbolism: Water has been widely used as a symbol of the subconscious mind, and nudity is an obvious symbol of feeling metaphorically "exposed" in front of others. Thus, Leggatt symbolically rises out of the Captain's subconscious, because he feels that he is "exposing" his weaknesses as a new commander. Note that when Leggatt first encounters the Captain, he asks, "I suppose your captain's turned in?" Leggatt assumes that the Captain is an ordinary seaman—perfectly understandable under the circumstances, but also a clear indication that there is nothing stately or "captain-like" about the Captain. Also note that the Captain first obliquely denies his position, saying that he is "sure" the captain isn't turned in, before he states, "I am the captain." Again, note that while he is technically the Captain, he lacks the qualities that suggest the *substance* of a captain, such as fortitude, presence, and strength. Conrad's story is, in part, about the Captain's acquisition of these qualities through the help of Leggatt.

Conrad begins stressing the idea that Leggatt is—in certain important ways—the Captain's double. His use of what is commonly called the *doppelganger theme* serves to highlight the qualities that the Captain lacks by showing them embodied in his double. Leggatt's being dressed in one of the Captain's sleeping suits and hiding in his cabin suggests their relationship in physical terms; but Conrad suggests their bond in many other ways as well: Both men are young, both hold (or, in Leggatt's case, held) posts of importance that they acquired through their "connections," both are "Conway boys," both are isolated from their respective crews, both save a ship during a dangerous event, and both eventually strike out for "new destinies." Each man offers something to his double: The Captain offers Leggatt a place to hide and his eventual means of escape, while Leggatt forces the Captain, through his assistance in helping him at Koh-ring, a chance to prove his seamanship in the eyes of the crew.

The fact that the Captain so readily believes Leggatt's story about his murder of the sailor may mark him as gullible or even foolish in the eyes of some. However, the Captain—although working with a crew—feels isolated from them, and welcomes Leggatt's presence in much the same way that Leggatt welcomes his. Leggatt is, at first, someone the Captain can speak to, and he offers to help him almost as a means of continuing their "secret" relationship. The *doppelganger theme* usually involves a man meeting what the Captain calls his "other self." In this light, Leggatt is (figuratively) a "part" of the Captain that he doesn't know he possesses. At the story's end, Leggatt has effectively opened the Captain's eyes to the qualities he thought he lacked at the beginning of his command. Thus, the Captain immediately offers to hide Leggatt because, in a *symbolic* sense, Leggatt *is* the Captain—or at least the part of him that has been, until now, unexpressed. The Captain's future meeting with the Skipper of the *Sephora* at the start of Part 2 is one of the first tests of this newly developing part of himself.

Glossary

(Here and in the following chapters, difficult words and phrases, as well as allusions and historical references, are explained.)

Gulf of Siam "Siam" is the old name of Thailand; the Gulf of Siam is the arm of the South China Sea, between the Malay and Indochinese peninsulas.

Cuddy the cook's galley on a small ship.

Cardiff seaport in Southeast Wales, on the Bristol Channel; capital of Wales and county seat of South Glamorgan.

Malay Archipelago large group of islands between Southeast Asia and Australia, including Indonesia, the Philippines, and sometimes New Guinea.

beyond my ken beyond my range of knowledge.

Binnacle the upright, cylindrical stand holding a ship's compass, usually located near the helm.

Conway boy sailor who trained on the British battleship Conway.

Norfolk county of East England, on the North Sea.

Ratlines any of the small, relatively thin pieces of tarred rope that join the shrouds of a ship and serve as the steps of a ladder for climbing the rigging. "Shrouds" are sets of ropes or wires stretched from a ship's side to a masthead to offset lateral strain on the mast.

Mizzen the mast that is third from the bow of a ship with three or more masts. (The "bow" is the front part of a ship.)

gimbals a pair of rings pivoted on axes at right angles to each other so that one is free to swing within the other; a ship's compass, pelorus, and so on, will remain horizontal at all times when suspended in gimbals.

Java Head the westernmost point of Java, a large island of Indonesia, southeast of Sumatra.

Halter hangman's noose.

Cain in the Bible, the oldest son of Adam and Eve; he killed his brother Abel.

Bullock a young bull.

Square the yards by lifts and braces nautical command meaning, "Sail directly before the wind." "Yards" are slender rods or spars, tapering toward the ends and fastened at right angles across a mast to support a sail; "braces" are ropes passed through blocks at the ends of yards, used to swing the yard about from the deck.

Part 2

Summary

The Skipper of the *Sephora* arrives on board the Captain's ship, look-ing for any sign of Leggatt. The Skipper is distressed over Leggatt's actions and disappearance, explaining that he has been at sea for thirty-seven years and has never seen anything like what happened with Leggatt.

The Captain offers the Skipper the explanation that perhaps the heavy sea—rather than Leggatt—killed the crewman, but the Skipper tells him that this could not have been the case. He then tells the Captain that he will have to report Leggatt as a suicide.

The Skipper is, however, suspicious of the Captain and remarks that while the mainland is seven miles away, the Captain's ship is only two miles away from the *Sephora*. To mislead the Skipper, the Captain shows him the rest of his cabin and stateroom, announcing his intention to do so, so that Leggatt will know to remain absolutely still. As the Skip-per descends the ladder to return to his ship, he begins to ask the Captain if he suspects Leggatt to be on board, but the Captain quickly dismisses him with, "Certainly not."

The Captain and Leggatt have another secret conversation. Leggatt tells the Captain that the *Sephora's* Skipper lied when he said that he gave the order to repair the foresail. Rather, he whimpered about their "last hope" while Leggatt repaired the foresail without being told to do so. The Captain, wholly convinced of Leggatt's innocence, understands that the weather, on the night Leggatt killed the crewman, "crushed an unworthy mutinous existence."

Leggatt's presence in the Captain's cabin causes the Captain to con-stantly think of him, and the Chief Mate and the helmsman notice the Captain behaving in an odd, stealthy manner. The Captain's tension grows more unbearable. During this time, Leggatt hides mostly in the Captain's bathroom and sleeps with him in his bed. Leggatt eats tins of preserves stored in the Captain's locker and drinks the Captain's morn-ing coffee.

Leggatt asks the Captain to maroon him on a nearby shore, since he will not return to England to be tried and hung. The Captain initially refuses, but then agrees to grant Leggatt his wish.

At midnight, the Captain goes on deck and orders this ship to change its tack and approach the east side of the Gulf. The Chief Mate silently hints at his disapproval and tells the Second Mate that the order shows a lack of judgment. By noon, the Chief Mate wonders when the Captain will order a change of course. However, the Captain tells him that they will be sailing as close to the islands as they can to find some "land breezes" to propel them more quickly than they were moving in the middle of the Gulf. The Chief Mate expresses his shock at this decision.

That night, the Captain tells Leggatt that he will steer the ship near Koh-ring, an island that seems inhabited. The Captain will maneuver the ship to within half a mile of the shore. Leggatt warns him to be careful, lest a mishap cost the Captain his first command.

The Captain returns to the deck and orders the Second Mate to open the quarter-deck ports. He then returns to his cabin and tells Leggatt to escape out of the quarter-deck ports while the rest of the crew is occupied. He also tells him to lower himself to the sea with a rope to avoid a splash. Leggatt grabs the Captain's arm as a silent gesture of thanks.

That night, the Captain visits Leggatt for the last time. He gives him three sovereigns, which Leggatt initially refuses but eventually accepts. Neither man says anything when they separate for the last time.

When the Captain returns to the deck, he is startled by the ship's proximity to the land, but he knows he must maintain this course to help Leggatt escape. He orders the helmsman to continue their course, while the other crewmen stare in disbelief. They approach Koh-ring, and as the ship gets closer to the land, the members of the crew begin vocalizing their concern. The Chief Mate cries that the ship's bottom will be torn off by the land and the helmsman expresses his doubts over the Captain's order to maintain their course.

Although the Captain remains stern to the men, he is filled with doubt about their chances of survival. The dark sky, combined with the shadow of the hills of Koh-ring make navigation very difficult, and the Captain wishes he had some kind of mark in the water by which to gage his steering. Suddenly, he sees a white object in the water within a yard of the ship's side—he recognizes it as his hat, which he gave to Leggatt and which had fallen off his head when he began his swim to shore. The Captain uses this mark to help him steer the ship, which avoids being grounded and steers clear of any further danger. The Captain now feels in perfect command of the ship and his crew. As his ship sails on, he watches his hat disappear from view and thinks of Leggatt, "striking out for a new destiny."

Commentary

Literary Device

Conrad suggests that Leggatt "shares" his better qualities with the Captain; he also uses the Skipper of the *Sephora* to contrast the kind of captain that the Captain will become at the end of the story. The *Sephora's* Skipper represents one possible outcome of the Captain's fate, as does Leggatt. The Skipper is a man who hides behind his command, fearful of any damage to his reputation and fearful of his own crew. (The presence of his wife on board may be a hint that the Skipper is more "wimpy" than he should be when commanding the *Sephora*.) Recall Leggatt's story in Part 1: Although the Skipper knew that Leggatt saved the ship by repairing the foresail, he would not allow this to mitigate Leggatt's punishment because "He was afraid of the men, and also of that old second mate of his." Like the Captain, the Skipper was faced with a second mate who questioned his command—but unlike the Captain during the episode at Koh-ring, he is too afraid of looking foolish in front of others to give any order that may seem questionable. The Skipper also lies to the Captain about the foresail, saying he ordered its repair, when in fact Leggatt was responsible for doing the job and saving the *Sephora*. Fearful of giving any credit to Leggatt, the Skipper lies to mask his own lack of foresight, seamanship, and conviction. He also tells the Captain that he "never liked" Leggatt—but according to Leggatt, the Skipper was unable to meet his eyes when visiting him in his cabin, suggesting the guilt felt by the Skipper over arresting Leggatt for a technical, yet accidental, crime. The kind of command practiced by the Skipper is exactly what Leggatt helps the Captain avoid.

Theme

Part 2 also marks the Captain's growing bravery, which is contrasted with the Skipper's cowardice. When speaking to the Skipper, the Captain tells him he is hard of hearing so that the Skipper will speak loud enough for Leggatt to hear him; and he deftly handles the Skipper's attempts at prying information about Leggatt out of him. Note that

as the Captain continues risking his command for Leggatt, their relationship takes a physical toll on him: He stealthily paces the decks,
startles the steward, and must force himself to adopt the "unconscious
alertness" required of all able seamen. While Leggatt teaches the Captain what makes a good commander, the lessons are exhausting and
trying. As the Captain says, this period is "an infinitely miserable time."

Leggatt himself becomes even more unreal in the second half of the
story. During the scene where the steward almost discovers Leggatt in
the Captain's bathroom, the Captain wonders if Leggatt is "not visible
to other eyes" than his own. He forms an "irresistible doubt" of Leggatt's bodily existence and even compares keeping the secret to being
haunted. Even Leggatt is aware of his ghost-like status when he tells the
Captain, "It would never do for me to come to life again." Unlike the
keeper of a haunted house, however, the Captain is haunted by his other
self, which is by the presence of a man who, the Captain comes to realize, embodies the part of him that needs to be revealed if he is to mature
as a commander and not become a doddering coward, such as the Skipper of the *Sephora*.

This crucial distinction is made clear to the Captain when Leggatt
tells him that he must maroon him. At first, the Captain resists, stating
that they "are not living a boy's adventure story" and that such a plan
is absurd. Leggatt, ever the teacher, tells the Captain that he thought
he had "understood thoroughly," which makes the Captain consider
the shaping of his own personality.

Being able to recognize his own cowardice frees the Captain from
acquiring the cowardice so obvious in the Skipper of the *Sephora*.

The Captain's maneuvering of the ship at Koh-ring stands as the
ultimate test of his newly discovered traits. At first, the Chief Mate questions his decision to "stand right in," that is, to take the ship close to
the islands to pick up the land breezes. "Bless my soul!" the Chief Mate
cries. "Do you mean, sir, in the dark amongst the lot of all them islands
and reefs and shoals?" The Captain finds a new assurance in his voice
(unlike when first speaking to Leggatt) and says, "It's got to be Koh-
ring." This assurance is even more pronounced when he is questioned
by the Second Mate about opening the quarter-deck ports and responds,
"The only reason you need concern yourself about is because I tell you
to do so." Earlier in Part 2, the Captain notices Leggatt's complete *sanity*, and it is this sanity, or ability to remain level-headed in times of dis-
tress, that the Captain has effectively "borrowed" from Leggatt.

The Captain and Leggatt's parting conveys the degree to which each man has assisted the other. The Captain tells Leggatt, "I hope I have understood," to which Leggatt replies, "You have. From first to last." Like a student at a graduation ceremony, the Captain receives his "diploma" from his teacher, Leggatt. The men are then silent as Leggatt grasps his savior's arm. They have grown close enough that words would only be superfluous.

Character Insight

The story's final scene reflects the degree to which the Captain has changed due to his relationship with Leggatt. The Captain's words to his crew become more forceful and direct. Strong commands, such as, "Keep her full," "Don't check her way," "Turn all hands up," and "Be quiet," pepper his speech, and when the Chief Mate babbles in fear (like the Skipper of the *Sephora*), the Captain grabs his arm and shakes it "violently." Although he, too, is afraid to look at the land, he refuses to betray his own doubts to the men he commands.

When he sees his white hat floating in the sea, left by Leggatt as he began his swim to safety, the Captain is able to steer the ship away from the island and back into safer waters. The fact that the Captain's *own* hat serves as his mark reiterates the idea that Leggatt is that "secret" part of *himself* that even he did not know existed. After the ship moves out of danger, the Captain feels "the perfect communion of a seaman with his first command." As he thinks of Leggatt being free, the proud swimmer striking out on a new destiny, these words apply to the Captain as well. The Captain is now free from his own timidity; he is proud, as he metaphorically swims to his future as a commander; and he is striking out on a new destiny as well as a man who has discovered a previously hidden part of himself.

Glossary

bo's'n phonetic spelling of "boatswain," a ship's warrant officer or petty officer in charge of the deck crew, the rigging, anchors, boats, and so on.

campstool a lightweight, folding stool.

Cambodge Cambodian.

What does the Bible say? 'Driven from the face of the earth.' in the story of Cain and Abel, Cain complains he will be "driven from the face of the earth" for the murder of his brother.

Koh-ring the prefix "Koh" connotes an island; the island of Koh-ring is Conrad's creation.

Cochin-China historic region and former French colony in Southeast Indochina; the southern part of Vietnam.

that unplayful cub the second mate; a "cub" is an inexperienced, awkward youth.

Sunda Straits straits running between a group of islands in the Malay Archipelago, consisting of two smaller groups; Greater Sunda Islands (Sumatra, Java, Borneo, Sulawesi, and small nearby islands) and Lesser Sunda Islands (Bali and islands stretching east through Timor).

a bark of the dead floating in slowly under the very gate of Erebus a boat leading departed souls to Erebus, the dark place under the earth where the dead pass before entering Hades, according to Greek mythology.

mainyard the lowest yard on the mainmast (the principal mast of a vessel),from which the mainsail is set. (A "yard" is a slender rod or spar, tapering toward the ends and fastened at right angles across a mast to support a sail.)

taffrail the rail around the stern of a ship. (The "stern" is the back end of a ship.)

the poop on sailing ships, a raised deck at the stern, sometimes forming the roof of a cabin.

"She's round" the ship has passed around the land and is clear of danger.

foreyards the lowest yards on the foremast (the mast nearest the bow, or front, of a ship), from which the foresail is set. (A "yard" is a selnder rod or spar, tapering toward the ends and fastened at right angles across a mast to support a sail.)

CHARACTER ANALYSES

The Captain

Appointed to the command of his ship only a fortnight before the story begins, the Captain is a young and inexperienced, sincere yet uninspiring commander who eventually learns to call upon his previously hidden reserves of strength and cunning. In the beginning of the story, his authority is undermined slightly by his sneering second mate. He offers to take the anchor-watch himself to learn about the ship and feel less alienated. Early in the story, he states, "My position was that of the only stranger on board," and, more significantly, "I was somewhat of a stranger to myself." His feeling out-of-place on the ship mirrors his feelings of inadequacy concerning his new command.

After he meets Leggatt, however, the Caption begins behaving in ways that surprise both himself and his crew. He becomes more daring (constantly maneuvering Leggatt to prevent his discovery), more cunning (lying to the *Sephora's* Skipper about being hard-of-hearing), and more courageous (steering the ship close enough to Koh-ring so that Leggatt can swim to safety). He begins commanding his men in a direct and unapologetic way, and eventually wins their respect by keeping his composure during the episode at Koh-ring. This change in the Captain is what drives the story forward until its end, when he feels "the perfect communion of a seaman with his first command."

Leggatt

The ex-Chief Mate of the *Sephora*, Leggatt is an impulsive man who acts according to his own sense of justice rather than any formalized regulations that attempt to draw a line between right and wrong. While he did kill a man aboard the *Sephora*, he did so unintentionally after the two became embroiled in a brawl. Because he knows, however, that no judge will spare him the gallows, he decides to escape his confinement on the *Sephora* and to risk his life searching for a "new destiny."

Conrad draws attention to one of Leggatt's qualities in particular upon his entrance into the story — his physical strength. After being discovered by the Captain (hanging onto the rope ladder), Leggatt informs him that he previously swam to an islet and then to the Captain's ship—a distance of two miles. Conrad's attention to the detail of

Leggatt's physical strength reflects his emotional strength as well. Determined never to face an "old fellow in a wig and twelve respectable tradesmen" in court, Leggatt escapes his bondage, fakes his own death, and at the story's end, strikes out for freedom. His strength is inspiring to the Captain, who begins a "secret sharing" of Leggatt's better qualities as the story proceeds.

The Skipper of the *Sephora*

While Leggatt is resolute and self-determined, the Skipper of the *Sephora* is a weak, doddering man who hides behind the law to appease his conscience. After Leggatt's murder of the insolent sailor, the Skipper pronounces, "Mr., Leggatt, you have killed a man. You can no longer act as chief mate of this ship." This seems to be a reasonable (and necessary) pronouncement, but Conrad reveals another side of the Skipper when he portrays his visit to Leggatt's room. The Skipper looks "sick" and cannot look Leggatt in the face, for he feels ashamed because he is bringing Leggatt to his certain execution despite the fact that he single-handedly saved the *Sephora* during the storm. Rather than take a moral stand and allow Leggatt to escape, however, the Skipper retreats to the letter of the law. The fact that he tells Leggatt, "I represent the law here" while he is trembling reveals his cowardice and lack of conviction. As Leggatt explains, the Skipper is "afraid of the men, and also of that old second mate of his." The Skipper's weakness is further seen when he attempts to interrogate the Captain about Leggatt in a roundabout way, only to be easily tricked into believing that Leggatt has drowned.

The Second Mate

Although he is a minor character, the Captain's second mate serves to illustrate the lack of respect the crew feels toward the Captain. When the Captain first sights the *Sephora* and asks his crew if they know anything about it, the second mate looks down and smirks, as if in disbelief at the Captain's ignorance. This upsets the Captain, who notes, "It was not my part to encourage sneering on my ship," but he still feels unable to do anything about it.

The Chief Mate

Like the second mate, the Captain's chief mate is another minor character on board the ship who doubts the Captain's ability to command. Although not a "sneering" man such as the second mate, the chief mate does express great doubt and fear about the Captain's actions at Koh-ring, causing the Captain to order him to "Be quiet." After the episode at Koh-ring, however, the Captain has sufficiently proven his worth to the crew, forever stifling the objections of the chief and second mates.

CRITICAL ESSAYS

"The Secret Sharer" as Allegory

An *allegory* is a work of art in which characters and events take on metaphorical or symbolic meanings that are deliberately cultivated by the artist. The most famous literary allegory in English is John Bunyan's *Pilgrim's Progress* (1678), where symbolic characters (with names such as Christian, Evangelist, and Faithful) move through a symbolic plot (part of which, for example, involves their fleeing the City of Destruction) to arrive at the Celestial City eventually. Bunyan's allegory is clear and straightforward: Any person who wishes to reach Heaven must remain pure despite all of the hardships and tests he will face. Another widely known allegory is Edmund Spenser's *The Faerie Queen* (1590) in which different knights represent different virtues, such as holiness, temperance, and chastity. Because of their accessibility and moral teachings, allegories have been popular with readers since the beginnings of English literature.

While "The Secret Sharer" may not seem as obviously allegorical as the aforementioned works, it can nonetheless be read as an allegorical examination of a timid man becoming more daring and therefore, more complete. The primary allegorical element in the story is its plot: As the Captain journeys through the Gulf of Siam and eventually to within the shadow of Koh-ring, he also undertakes a metaphorical journey within himself. Just as a traveler is in a different place literally at the end of a journey, so the Captain is in a different emotional "place" as he watches Leggatt swim to shore.

Conrad's depiction of the Captain also invites the reader to consider the story's other allegorical implications. For example, the young and inexperienced Captain wants to behave in a resolute and forthright manner, but he lacks the courage and sense of command that would enable him to do so. Conrad's making the Captain the newly appointed commander of a ship on foreign seas evokes those situations in every person's life when he or she is called upon to show courage and steadfastness, but feels out of place and uncomfortable with such demands.

Leggatt's appearance changes all this. In terms of the allegory, Leggatt is like the scorpion that smuggled its sway into the Chief Mate's inkwell: sly, inexplicable, and potentially deadly. The fact that Leggatt killed a man—however accidentally or unintentionally—suggests his symbolic position as the more brutal, impulsive part of the human psyche. His initial nudity suggests his symbolically elemental essence in all of us: He is naked because he represents the human soul "stripped down" to its essentials without being "disguised" in any guise. When the Captain offers Leggatt one of his sleeping suits, the allegorical implications are unmistakable: Leggatt *is*—symbolically—a part of the Captain that readers see at the end of his "voyage."

Another piece of clothing that holds allegorical significance is the Captain's hat, which he gives to Leggatt before allowing him to escape the ship and swim to Koh-ring's shores. The last third of the story, when the Captain maneuvers the ship next to Koh-ring, repeatedly depicts the island as a symbol of death, looming over the Captain and his (understandably) terrified crew. However, to grow as a person (so Conrad's allegory goes), the Captain must experience a "brush with death" to test his newfound confidence. If not for Leggatt's losing the Captain's hat, which the Captain then uses to help him steer clear of the shoals, the ship would certainly be destroyed. This clarifies the plot. But in terms of the allegory, the hat suggests something else: Despite his having been assisted by Leggatt in finding his confidence and bravery, ultimately, the Captain *himself* is responsible for his transformation—a proposition that accords with the notion of Leggatt symbolically representing a part of the Captain's personality. Thus, the Captain's own hat saves his ship because it is the Captain himself who grows as a person and is responsible for his own change.

The Skipper of the *Sephora* enters the allegorical equation as well. As Leggatt symbolically represents the more passionate and dangerous side of man, the Skipper represents a side even more timid than the Captain at the beginning of the story. For example, he refuses to take a stand to help Leggatt, despite that the man Leggatt killed was an insolent sailor who could have cost all the men their lives *and* despite the fact that Leggatt killed the man accidentally. Thus, Conrad begins "The Secret Sharer" with the Captain being offered two extreme modes of behavior: Leggatt's and the Skipper's. The Captain encounters each one physically and emotionally, but by the end of the story, he has completed his allegorical journey through the symbolic shadow of death and looks forward, as does his symbolic counterpart, to a "new destiny."

Finally, the story's title reflects its overall allegory of growth and change. The Captain conceals Leggatt because—like many people—he tries to stifle and keep down the more physical and dangerous part of himself. He would rather possess a façade of cool control than fall prey to his own violent impulses. However, the story suggests that there are times in a person's life when he must call upon his "Leggatt" side to complete a dangerous task or prove himself worthy of his hire. We are all "secret sharers" of our darker selves, but we all keep them in reserve for use in dire situations.

"The Secret Sharer" and *Heart of Darkness:* A Comparative Analysis

Conrad's work—like that of many great writers—sometimes explores similar themes in similar ways. "The Secret Sharer" and *Heart of Darkness* intersect in numerous ways, overlapping, and exploring similar ideas.

Both works feature a first-person narrator who undergoes a physical journey (through the Gulf of Siam and up the Congo River, respectively) that mirrors the more intense and emotional journey that occurs inside of him as he gets closer to the journey's end. As the Captain approaches Koh-ring, he learns a great deal about his fears, his capabilities, and the means by which he can confront and defeat them. Similarly, as Marlow creeps towards Kurtz, he is forced to re-evaluate his ideas about indigenous peoples, civilization, and the metaphorical darkness within himself. An important difference between these characters is that at the end of "The Secret Sharer," the Captain is poised and confident, while at the end of *Heart of Darkness*, Marlow is broken and morally exhausted.

As mentioned in the Introduction to "The Secret Sharer," the story uses the *doppelganger* theme to illustrate the duality of the Captain's character. The meeting of the Captain and Leggatt is like an allegorical meeting of timidity and rashness. To resolve this duality, the Captain must "use" a small amount of Leggatt's rashness to help him escape, and, in a larger sense, help himself lose some of his own unease and apprehension. The Captain is grateful to Leggatt for helping him discover his capacity for bravery.

In *Heart of Darkness*, however, Marlow faces a much more sinister and disturbing double. Kurtz is a methodical and cold-blooded killer, who embodies all of the Company's sins as well as the symbolic "heart of darkness" that is potentially present in even the most "civilized" of men. Unlike the Captain, who embraces the courage displayed by Leggatt, Marlow retreats from the horror he sees in Kurtz. For the rest of his life, Marlow will be troubled by what Kurtz revealed about the capacity for evil that may exist in every man.

Like *Heart of Darkness*, "The Secret Sharer," features a number of symbols to focus the reader's attention on the work's chief issues and ideas. The scorpion is a symbol of an evil outcast, attempting to stow himself away and avoid detection—which is exactly how Leggatt is initially presented to the reader. The Captain's sleeping suit (that he lends to Leggatt) symbolizes the "secret sharing" that occurs between the two men. He black shadow of Koh-ring is an ominous symbol of death, looming before the Captain as he attempts to prove his seamanship. Finally, the Captain's white hat, left in the sea by Leggatt, symbolizes the Captain's desire to protect Leggatt as well as Leggatt's assistance of the Captain.

Both works' titles become more meaningful and complex as the works proceed. The title "The Secret Sharer" initially refers to the Captain with whom Leggatt shares the secret of his escape from the *Sephora*. However, as the story progresses, the title also refers to Leggatt, with whom the Captain "shares" *his* "secret" of timidity and fear. Conrad's device of making the title apply to both men is particularly apt, because both men benefit from the sharing of their respective secrets with the other: Leggatt gains his freedom from prison and the Captain gains his freedom from the "prison" of his lack of self-assurance.

Likewise, *Heart of Darkness* initially refers to the geographical place to which Marlow voyages when he works for the Company. As the novel progresses, the reader understands that the absence of an article in the title also refers to the metaphorical "heart of darkness" potentially inside all people. This complexity grows until the end of the novel, when the anonymous narrator looks at the Thames and says that it seems to lead "into the heart of an immense darkness." Africa is no longer the only "dark place" on the earth; instead, the "heart of darkness" is close and only a metaphorical boat ride away.

CLIFFSNOTES REVIEW

Use this CliffsNotes Review to test your understanding of the original text and reinforce what you've learned in this book. After you work through the review and essay questions, identify the quote section, and the fun and useful practice projects, you're well on your way to understanding a comprehensive and meaningful interpretation of "The Secret Sharer."

Q & A

1. What was the chief mate surprised to find in his room?

   a. a scorpion

   b. a beetle

   c. a snake

   d. a black cat

2. Which of the following things do Leggatt and the Captain have in common?

   a. their age

   b. their training

   c. their family connections

   d. all of the above

3. The Captain helps Leggatt avoid detection by the *Sephora's* Skipper by

   a. pretending to be hard-of-hearing

   b. refusing to allow the Skipper on board

   c. hiding Leggatt in a barrel

   d. having Leggatt pose as one of his crew

Answers: (1) a. (2) d. (3) a.

Identify the Quote

1. "But what I felt most was my being a stranger to the ship; and if all the truth must be told, I was somewhat of a stranger to myself."

2. "My father's a parson in Norfolk."

3. "I have been at sea now, man and boy, for seven-and-thirty years, and I've never heard of such a thing happening in an English ship. And that it should be my ship. Wife on board, too."

4. "She will never get out. You have done it, sir. I knew it'd end something like this. She will never weather, and you are too close now to stay. She'll drift ashore before she's round. O my God!"

5. ". . . a free man, a proud swimmer striking out for a new destiny."

Answers: (1) The Captain, describing to the reader his initial unease at his new command. (2) Leggatt, when he first tells his story to the Captain. (3) The Skipper of the *Sephora*, as he searches the Captain's ship for Leggatt. (4) The chief mate to the Captain, as the ship nears Koh-ring. (5) The Captain, dscribing Leggatt to the reader at the very end of the story.

Essay Questions

1. Trace how the Captain's character changes by concealing Leggatt.

2. Discuss Conrad's use of the *doppelganger* theme in both "The Secret Sharer" and *Heart of Darkness*.

3. Describe the allegorical meaning of the story.

4. Explain how both "The Secret Sharer" and *Heart of Darkness* treat the theme of knowledge. What, for example, are some of the different kinds of knowledge learned by the characters in both works?

Practice Projects

1. Read Edgar Allan Poe's story, "William Wilson," and compose a dialogue between Poe's narrator and the Captain that discusses what they have learned from their "doubles."

Consult reference sources on Sigmund Freud's ideas about the conscious mind, specifically his ideas about the id, ego, and superego. Consider how Freud's ideas can be applied to "The Secret Sharer" and then create a poster on which you compare Conrad and Freud's ideas about the make-ups of our personalities. (Freud's *The Interpretation of Dreams* is a good starting point for your research.)

CLIFFNOTES RESOURCE CENTER

The learning doesn't need to stop here. CliffsNotes Resource Center shows you the best of the best—links to the best information in print and online about the author and/or related works. And don't think that this is all we've prepared for you; we've put all kinds of pertinent information at www.cliffsnotes.com. Look for all the terrific resources at your favorite bookstore or local library and on the Internet. When you're online, make your first stop www.cliffsnotes.com where you'll find more incredibly useful information about *Heart of Darkness* and "The Secret Sharer."

Books

This CliffsNotes book provides a meaningful interpretation of *Heart of Darkness* and "The Secret Sharer" published by Hungry Minds, Inc. If you are looking for information about the author and/or related works, check out these other publications:

BATCHELOR, JOHN. *Joseph Conrad: A Critical Biography.* Cambridge, Massachusetts; Blackwell Publishers, 1994. Batchelor's book is a combination of biography and criticism that examines some of the ways that Conrad's literary output helped him satisfy his psychological needs.

HOCHSCHILD, ADAM. *King Leopold's Ghost: A Story of Greed, Terror, and Heroism in Colonial Africa.* New York; Houghton Mifflin Company, 1998. This harrowing and shocking book traces King Leopold II's colonization of the Congo and the genocide that occurred there. Hochschild also offers biographies of figures who Conrad may have used for Kurtz. This book is essential reading for any student desiring to know more about the setting of *Heart of Darkness.*

MEYERS, JEFFREY. *Joseph Conrad: A Biography.* New York; Charles Scribner's Sons, 1991. Meyers's readable biography focuses, in part, on Conrad's Polish roots, his friendships with other writers, and some of the real-life models for his characters.

SCHWARZ, DANIEL, ed. *The Secret Sharer: A Complete Authoritative Text with Biographical and Historical Contexts, Critical History, and Essays from Five Contemporary Critical Perspectives.* Boston: Bedford

Books, 1997. This book's title summarizes its contents; in it, a reader will find information about how Conrad's life affected the writing of the story and modern interpretations of the story's themes.

Internet

Check out these Web resources for more information about Joseph Conrad and/or related works.

Bazter, Gisele. Notes on Joseph Conrad's *Heart of Darkness*. University of British Columbia. 28 October 1999 www.interhcange.ubc.ca/gmb/conrad.html. This site offers Professor Baxter's notes on several key aspects of the novel, including its style and its presentation of Kurtz. She also offers a section of study questions and links to other Conrad-based sites.

Blackmask Online. This site features e-texts of both *Heart of Darkness* and "The Secret Sharer." www.Blackmask.com.

Bradley, Candace. Africa and Africans in *Heart of Darkness*. Lawrence University. 24 January 1996 www.lawrence.edu/fac/bradleyc/heart.html. A site featuring Bradley's lecture on the portrayal of Africa in Conrad's novel from an anthropologist's perspective, the site also contains links to other lectures on Conrad.

Csicseri, Coreen. *Heart of Darkness*. The University at Buffalo www.acsu.buffalo.edu/~csicseri/. This site is a good starting point for an online investigation of Conrad. It offers a hypertext version of the novel, as well as links to pages on the novel's themes and major characters.

Crook, Tim. A Radio Adaptation of *Heart of Darkness*. Independent Radio Drama Productions, Ltd.; August 1989. www.irdp.co.uk/darkness.htm. This site features a passage of (and links to) the entire text of Crook's fascinating adaptation of the novel. In this version, Crook intertwines the voices of Marlow, Conrad, and Kurtz as the plot unfolds, creating a multi-layered running commentary on the novel's plot and ideas.

Kill Devil Hill. This site features a number of bulletin-board discussion sites devoted to various authors, including Conrad. www.Killdevilhill.com There are messages posted about both *Heart of Darkness* and "The Secret Sharer."

Films and Other Recordings

The films, audio tapes, and adaptations listed below can give you an even greater understanding of Conrad's *Heart of Darkness*.

Apocalypse Now. Dir. Francis Ford Coppola. With Martine Sheen, Robert Duvall, and Marlon Brando. United Artists, 1979. Coppola's adaptation of *Heart of Darkness* set during the Vietnam War follows the journey of Captain Willard (the Marlow figure) who searches for Colonel Walter Kurtz in Cambodia. This controversial film contains numerous parallels to Conrad's novel.

Heart of Darkness and the Congo Diary, by Joseph Conrad. Audiotape. Read by David Threlfall. Penguin USA, 1994. This is one of the many audio versions of the novel available on audio cassette.

Heart of Darkness. Dir. Nicolas Regg. With Tim Roth and John Malkovich. Turner Home Video, 1994. This made-for-TV film of the novel is a more "straightforward" adaptation than *Apocalypse Now.*

Hearts of Darkness. Dir. Fax Bahr and Eleanor Coppola. With Martin Sheen, Francis Ford Coppola, Eleanor Coppola, Dennis Hopper and John Millius. Paramount Home Video, 1991. This film is a documentary about the making of *Apocalypse Now*, detailing how the film went far beyond its original shooting schedule and budget, causing a number of problems for almost everyone involved with its creation. The film features a number of interviews with members of the cast and crew.

Send Us Your Favorite Tips

In your quest for knowledge, have you ever experienced that sublime moment when you figure out a trick that saves time or trouble? Perhaps you realized you were taking ten steps to accomplish something that could have taken two. Or you found a little-known workaround that achieved great results. If you've discovered a useful tip that helped you understand the novels more effectively and you'd like to share it, the CliffsNotes staff would love to hear from you. Go to our Web site at www.cliffsnotes.com and click the Talk to Us button. If we select your tip, we may publish it as part of CliffsNotes Daily, our exciting, free e-mail newsletter. To find out more or to subscribe to a newsletter, go to www.cliffsnotes.com on the Web.

Index

NOTES

NOTES